The Witches' Key to the Legion

A Guide to Solomonic Sorcery

Editor: Laurelei Black

Author: Laurelei Black

Illustrators: Natalie Black and John Birkel

Cover Design: John Birkel

The Witches' Key to the Legion: A Guide to Solomonic Sorcery

ISBN: 978-0-9857734-2-7

Keywords

1. Goetia 2. Legion 3. Solomonic Magic 4. Witchcraft

The Witches' Key to the Legion

A Guide to Solomonic Sorcery

Adapted from the Lesser Key of Solomon the King, the Goetia

Edited and Revised by Laurelei Black
Illustrated by Natalie Black and John Birkel

ASTERIA
BOOKS

The Witches' Key to the Legion
A Guide to Solomonic Sorcery

Preface

γοητεία <u>goēteia</u> – charm, jugglery

γόης <u>goes</u> – charmer, enchanter, sorcerer

δαίμων <u>daemon</u> – nature spirit

δαίω <u>daio</u> – to divide (destinies)

θεουργία <u>theurgia</u> – high magick

For our purposes and work, I have little or no particular concern with theurgy – the "high magic" that many modern mages say is the purpose and aim of the magical life. Aleister Crowley, unarguably the most widely read editor of previous editions of *The Lesser Key of Solomon* (the Goetia), valued the practice of theurgy far above goetia and embedded many inclusions into his edition of the Key with the likely intention of elevating the magician beyond the "low magic" of goetia.

Please don't misunderstand. I have no issue with theurgic magic. It is good and proper in its place and time. I just have no desire to obscure the potency and availability of goetic magic. We are Witches – weavers of "Grey Magic" which blends the high and the low within one vessel. We embrace our physical natures and experience, and we do not deny the physical realm or the Underworld their proper places in preference of the "upper" (or celestial) world.

In many cultures where shamanism is practiced, spiritual movement takes place in three planes, worlds, or realms. The three realms are the world Above (the sky, heaven, land of the gods, the celestial plane), the world Between (the land, middle-earth, place of the elemental gates, land of the nature spirits, the physical plane), and the world Below (the sea, the underworld, land of the dead, the demonic plane). It is within us, as Witches and weavers of the wyrd, that the upper and lower worlds mix.

Furthermore, I believe that my brother Crowley (for I do share fraternal bonds with him and the many esteemed members of the Ordo Templi Orientis) did no favors for the daemons in this book by popularizing their conjuration with the sort of abusive exorcisms and other rituals that he presents for public consumption. These spirits are not all monsters bent on evil deeds. The ones who are, you would be wisest never to call, even with the supposed aid of elevated magical structures. Torture and bondage, if you are indeed capable of binding these beings, have only wrought the effect of making many spirits resentful of interacting with us.

Natalie Black, my life and magical partner, and I undertook this work at the request of the spirits with whom we consort. Our greatest guide and teacher in this current work is a member of the Legion. She has communicated a wealth of wisdom – both practical and theoretical – via talking boards, automatic writing, and scrying. She has been friend and mentor to us, shining a light into the world of shades so that we might bring you accurate and useful insight into spirit work.

If you are familiar with prior editions of the Goetia, you will undoubtedly recognize some differences in the descriptions included in this "New Key." Here you see our guide's insight and knowledge and how it adds to the lore and practical partnerships offered by each spirit.

What you will not find in this book are repetitive rituals that sling threats and abuse upon the spirits. Many of the spirits here require a "firm hand and a strong Will," but they will actively resent being insulted, threatened, and tortured, as has happened for the last several centuries. Indeed, spirit torture has been the norm since the printing of the many medieval grimoires, and it is attributed to Solomon himself.

Did Solomon actually form the Legion and write a book concerning the control of these spirits? That is a doubtful historical scenario, and yet the lore among mages long ago established it as a sort of "Energetic Truth." Whether it is literally true or not, Solomon's involvement with the spirits of the Legion has been canonized to the point that even many of the spirits believe (and claim to "remember" it) as a fact. Because it is, at this point, as good as true from a spiritual/energetic perspective, we will be writing about Solomon in this capacity throughout this work.

Whether Solomon or other magicians who followed him by centuries were the initiators of spirit torture, it is clear that the spirits of the Legion have suffered too long at the hands of sadistic masters. Some of these spirits are now dangerous and shouldn't be called upon at all.

In this *Witches' Key*, we have explored the Legion as it exists today. With the help of our familiar spirits from within the ranks, we offer you descriptions of the spirits and their seals, practical advice for working with these beings, history and lore related to the creation of the Legion, and a complete Demonic DO NOT CALL List.

The short editorial essays that serve to complement this work ("On the All and the Adversary," etc.) arc discussions that came out of our exploration of the 72 spirits of the Legion. When we began this work, this information was largely unknown to us; and we will freely admit that we have no scholarly or academic means of verifying any of it. Every morsel was given to us directly from our guides within the Legion – most from one spirit, in particular.

This work might accurately be termed Unverified Personal Gnosis, except that there were always two of us (a channel and an operator) involved in the sessions. Furthermore, much of what was revealed to us has been revealed to others in varying degrees, as we have discovered since the inception of this work.

As always, you are at liberty to make your own judgments and test this information against your own practice. We encourage you to take Lon Milo Duquette's advice, though, in his treatment on the Goetia: "One who has never experienced a Goetic Evocation is not qualified to voice even the most educated opinion on the subject. It is one thing to be well-read on a subject; it is quite another to be part of the subject itself. " Put this information into practice, and judge for yourself.

We hope that the information contained herein will be of value to you in your magical practice.

Why Create a Key for Witches?

I have two main reasons for targeting this book to Witches and not, say, Ceremonial Magicians. The first is that every other book available on the Goetia is aimed at Ceremonial Magicians. They are edited by illustrious members of the Golden Dawn and the Ordo Templi Orientis, and they assume a certain familiarity with those working systems. The editorial essays and commentary are excellent in their scholarship; and they are, for the most part, wonderful resources for any magician. I especially recommend Lon Milo DuQuette's *Illustrated Goetia*. Our biggest complaint with these books is that they continue to advocate spirit torture.

My second reason for marketing this "new key" to Witches specifically is that Natalie and I both firmly believe that it has been the role of the Witch to summon and stir spirits as allies in magic since Witches first started practicing their Craft. We see evidence of that in folklore, trial records, art, and in our own magical development. What we don't see are good modern resources for the Witch in undertaking this task.

Natalie and I are both Witches, working independently and in a coven. We are also both professional psychic readers. One common thread that we have seen in our own lives, in our coven, and in the experience of our clients is that we humans are spiritual beings having a human experience. We are spirits enfleshed, and we walk within a world of ethereal spirits who act as guides, guardians, and aides to us, often whether we are aware of them or not. We have gotten on the talking board numerous times with family and friends to find a helpful spirit has been by their sides since childhood or adolescence.

People find comfort in knowing that they are not alone, even if they cannot see their circle of friends because they dwell in Spirit. More than that, Witches find companions in magic among the spirits familiar to them (spirit familiars). This current work is, we feel, a giant step forward for the practicing Witch in discovering the entities who inhabit the Unseen Realms and in uncovering the means to communicate and work with them.

On Goetic Magic and Communication

These 72 spirits are each quite adept at different sorts of magic, though you'll find enough overlap between spirits to be assured of meeting a spirit with whom you share enough affinity to work in a cordial capacity. We've tried to include enough tables and quick references to make narrowing the field easier.

There is literally no end to the work you can accomplish with the help of "your little daemon." Liberal sciences, necromancy, alchemy, art, foreign language, diplomacy, law, love – these spirits know all of the things that you want to know. The can make learning significantly easier. They love what you love and will help you pursue, protect, and promote those passions.

We're not here to persuade theurgists out of their high magic, but we do want to remind you that Goetia is, by definition, low magic. It is sorcery, witchcraft. You don't have to make it complicated unless that placates your sense of the Arte Magical.

Each spirit is an individual and will have his preferred method of working, as well. Some are chatty, others communicate with images. Some might like complicated ritual and arcane language, while many prefer simplicity. Some sing – all the time. They are as individual and quirky as the magicians who work with them.

These new descriptions are vital because they give the magician an accurate idea of who these spirits are in the New Aeon. However old the *Lemegeton* may be, we know that the descriptions of the spirits have persisted in a relatively unchanged state since the 17ᵗʰ Century. Everybody changes at least a little in 400 years, even spirits. Furthermore, some details weren't recorded accurately in the first place. (As an example, they were all originally described as inherently masculine, regardless of how anciently that spirit may have been worshipped as a Goddess.)

Communicate with your chosen spirit in whatever way makes the most sense. If he is verbal, use automatic writing or a talking board as you develop your clairaudient abilities. If she is visual, use a scrying mirror, cauldron, crystal ball, etc. Try trance, flying out, lucid dreaming, smoke/fire scrying; or simply try listening and looking for your spirit.

The Unseen World is not a separate place, distinct and untouched by This World. Beings of spirit and beings of flesh walk in both places. We ourselves are, ultimately, beings of spirit who are also beings of flesh. Spirits know that we inhabit both spaces at once. Mages and Witches should know this, as well.

On Psychology and Models of Magic

Sorcerers of all ranks and orders tend to approach magic in one of a handful of ways. None is particularly wrong, and none is necessarily right. What is helpful about understanding these working models is gaining an appreciation for your own approach, as well as being able to adapt the work of others to suit your outlook.

Psychological Model

As Lon Milo DuQuette would say, "[Magic] is all in your head. You just have no idea how big your head is." This model takes the stance that all magic affects the inner planes, and that daemons, angels, and other spirits are projections of the Self. This model falls easily in line with Jungian psychology and the exploration of archetypes as projections of the Collective Unconscious.

Spirit Model

Those working within the Spirit Model view daemons, angels, Gods, and Goddesses as distinct and separate individuals with lives and intentions of their own. They are not projections of the Mage, but exist independently of magicians.

Energy Model

The Energy Model of magic accepts that something exists outside of the observer, but doesn't claim to know precisely what it is. In this model, daemons and Gods are similar to elemental, thermodynamic, electromagnetic, or other types of energies. They are forces at work in the Universe that the sciences haven't been able to quantify and define yet.

Chaos Model

Chaos magicians use a liberal mix of all three previous models. They use whatever works in the moment, whatever method or outlook achieves results.

I operate fairly firmly in the Spirit Model, leaning toward Chaos. I have found that most Witches operate somewhere on a continuum between Spirit and Chaos. This book, then, is written almost entirely from the Spirit Model, a fact for which I make no apologies. Like all books, though, it is adaptable to meet your needs. Use, lose, or abuse our techniques and information as you see fit.

On Evocation, Invocation, and Banishing

This book presupposes a basic magical education that includes a firm understanding and application of Will, grounding, centering, shielding, basic evocation, and banishing techniques. If you don't feel adequately trained in these areas, please educate yourself before attempting to contact any of the Legion. We recommend works by Lon Milo DuQuette and Donald Michael Kraig, in particular, to bring you up to speed.

In terms of invoking the 72 spirits of the Legion, we simply don't recommend it. Invocation is essentially possession, and unless you've been working for a great while with a spirit and have a particular affinity, you may be asking for trouble.

In regards to evocation, we advocate complete dismissal of previous texts in which threats, binding, and torture by fire are called up in order to induce the spirits to appear before the mage and do his bidding. If you and the spirit don't have great enough affinity for each other, or if the spirit is too mischievous or angry for you to summon without the use of force, you're obviously better off leaving that spirit alone.

That isn't to say that every spirit will respond to softly-worded requests. Many of the Legion require a firm hand and a strong Will in a Master. You must be strong, but not abusive.

The relationship you are seeking is an old-fashioned one. The spirits of the Legion refer to magicians as "Masters," but they are not our slaves. They are more like servants or employees; and if we are very lucky, they might become friends. We tend to make contractual agreements with them, whether we realize it or not, for either short or long periods of time. A simple magical working is relatively short, whereas having a spirit become your familiar is quite a long relationship. In either case, you do the spirit a disservice if you treat it like a slave. It is older than you, often by millennia, and it is probably willing and happy to help you if you treat it decently.

In the event that you have summoned a spirit who won't leave on his own, you must know how to effectively banish. This next bit of advice should go without saying, but I'll include it anyway out of caution: Don't summon any of the spirits in this book unless you can make them go away, if necessary. (As a cautionary note: You really can't force any of the spirits on the DO NOT CALL list to do anything, including go away – unless you're Solomon, which you probably aren't. So just refrain from calling them.) Anything from a good, strong impromptu dismissal to a full Star Ruby or Lesser Banishing Ritual of the Pentagram will work great.

You will not find any specific words of evocation in this book. Blame our Traditional Craft leanings, I suppose. We fall into our own unique patterns, but they're individual to us and our spirits.

Our advice is to be polite, specific, brief, and firm in both your evocations and your banishings.

On Spheres and Pyramids

The truest working space of the Sorcerer is not a flat space marked on the ground with words and symbols. Mark the circle and triangle with the names of Gods and Angels if it improves your focus, but understand that you live and work in three physical dimensions (and more which aren't of a physical nature).

The Mage needs a sphere, not a circle, to stand within. She calls spirits into a pyramid, not a triangle. Enclose yourself and the entity on all sides for sure protection.

We find that most Witches already work within this paradigm, marking their circle in 2D space while visualizing and energizing it in 3D space. However, the concept bears repeating, in the event that readers haven't been exposed to this idea previously.

Again, I have no interest in becoming the maker of lasting ritual (at least not in regards to the Legion). Devise your own words. Use none at all. Rely on Will and vision. Or let the words come extemporaneously from your own sorcery.

Another point to consider is that not every spirit needs to be called into a Pyramid. Many of these spirits are helpful and benevolent. A great many were/are Gods, Orishas, and Loa. Most Witches would call such entities into the Circle (Sphere) with themselves, not outside of it in a spirit trap. If you truly honor and respect the spirit whom you are calling, it makes sense to call it into your sphere.

On Affinity between Spirit and Witch

Not every spirit in the Legion is a good fit for each Witch or Mage. Not only are some spirits dangerous and should be avoided, but many are simply incompatible for a given individual.

A Witch will have a number of potential spirits from whom she might choose. During the time that she is researching those spirits, they might also be observing her.

When a particularly strong attraction presents itself to a Master, this spirit is a natural candidate to become a familiar. Indeed, the spirit may already be acting in that capacity for the Witch, and the Witch needs only to recognize the spirit's presence.

Of course, more than one spirit may be available to you from the Legion, but it is important that you pay close attention to how well these spirits work with each other before you take on multiple working partnerships with various spirits. They don't all get along, after all, and to bring too many of them into your life is to court madness.

Generally, spirits who are listed next to each other are similar in nature or temperament. Also, spirits who do similar work tend to get along with each other.

It's more common to have guides and helping spirits who are under the command of the named spirits of the Legion than it is to work with multiples of the Goetia, though I've known several people who work happily with multiples.

On Care and Keeping of Familiars

The decision to have a familiar is not a unilateral one. A Witch does not simply choose a spirit from a list and then trap it within a seal, a bottle, or a figurine. A familiar is not a spiritual slave or a prisoner.

The relationship between master and familiar should be mutually beneficial. The familiar assists in magic, according to his abilities; and the Witch returns energy in the forms of gratitude, gifts, ritual, or something specific to the familiar. Spirits will often tell you specifically what they want if you just talk to them.

In the section titled "On the Creation of the Legion," I mention that the spirits don't really care about the metals that have previously been assigned to them. Those metals, and the associated ranks, have planetary alignments based on Crowley's *Liber 777* that can provide some point of reference for the Witch in better understanding the spirits. However, the correspondences in *777* do not always translate well into the system of Craft you may be practicing, and the spirits themselves feel ambivalent about the correspondences that Crowley linked to them.

Most familiar spirits want some sort of housing. This is often a jar or bottle. In the case of my daughter's familiar, he wanted a little house she had painted for a small plush frog. On the talking board, he said, "I been lookin' at you frog house." He told her he wanted it just as was – with the acorns spilling out of the door and the cast-off earrings, seashells, and bullet casings still sitting on top. All he asked was that she remove the toy frog's name and add his veve. (Her familiar is a loa known in New Orleans Voudon practices.)

The housing can also take the shape of a candle or a statue. Natalie's familiar wanted a black candle as his domain. Mine wanted a very specific blue sugar bowl. Just ask and they will be very clear, often asking for something you already own.

They almost all like offerings, as well, though the nature of the offerings varies greatly from spirit to spirit. Our coven familiar wants smoke, and she gave us a specific incense recipe that we were to make and burn for her. The familiar of one of our students wanted ashes. She didn't care what was burned to create the ash, as long as it was burned with the intention of giving it to her. Some like honey, mint candies, liquor, or other comestibles. Again, we recommend asking your spirit directly what he wants and how often he wants it.

On the All and the Adversary

Just to be clear, the "All" is the Supreme Being – the Universal Spirit that penetrates all things. It is the totality of existence. The Universe. When spirits talk of God, this is who they mean. Jehovah (JHVH) is a specific and finite being, despite his publicity to the contrary. He is part of the All, but the All includes so much more. Jehovah excludes, alienates, and abandons, whereas the All cannot.

JHVH means "I will be what I will be." More commonly, we see this interpreted as "I am that I am." Either way, any one of us could say the same of ourselves. I am, and I will be. So will you. Furthermore, we are eternal spirits, creator spirits. We are like Jehovah, insomuch as the name indicates.

The All is Light (and, I would argue, Love). It binds the Universe together with the force of attraction. Its opponent is equally real, however. The Shaitan, Satan, the Adversary is the opposite of All. It is the Great Nothing. It is that which does not have existence. It is Oblivion.

These great forces – God and Satan – are not merely myths designed to keep weak-minded, weak-willed sheep enslaved. They are the great poles of magnetic force in the Universe. Foolish is the Mage (or Witch) who ignores his great Opponent. Careless is the Master who doesn't recognize his great Ally!

Just as God is All, so is the Adversary many. If God is present in all that exists, Satan is present in all that does not. Within science, he is evidenced in black holes and dark matter. He is the absence of being.

In the traditional Goetia, Satan is called by the name Amaymon, and he is served by the most wrathful, violent, and hateful spirits. I have sorted them onto the DO NOT CALL list, and I urge you to heed this warning. These spirits seek your destruction, just as the Adversary seeks to unmake what is made.

You'll note, we hope, that Lucifer is not on that list. Not only is Lucifer not included in the 72 spirits of the Goetia, but his name is not synonymous with the Adversary, nor is he his servant. The Light-Bringer is an angel and is part of God, part of the All. His "fall from grace" was a willful turning away from a singular focus on the All in order to bring illumination and enlightenment to humanity.

I know that discussion of God and Satan is not common in modern magical texts, particularly in texts intended for Witches. Most of us believe there is no place for Satan in our Craft – that "he" simply doesn't exist. In a very real sense, that is accurate. That Which Isn't does not exist. However, there are spirits and people who serve this Nothing, and therein lies my cautionary note. The Legion believes in the existence of the Adversary.

On the Creation of the Legion

Other writers and magicians more leaned and scholarly than we pretend to be have dealt with the historical veracity of the texts variously known as *The Lesser Key of Solomon the King*, the *Clavicula Salomonis Regis*, the *Lemegeton*, or the *Goetia*. Our intention in putting forth this current work is not to disparage or diminish previous scholarship but to add a new voice to the conversation, to shed new light on this old topic.

Our information comes, not from the Academic's library, but from the Witch's sphere and pyramid. We've talked with several of the 72 spirits in great depth. One is my familiar. Another is a close companion of Natalie. Where the creation of the Legion is concerned, most of our information comes directly from Astaroth. (Quite without coincidence, the medieval manuscript that became the *Key of Solomon* quite clearly states that Astaroth can tell the Mage how the Legion was created and bound.)

Here is what she told us:

Astaroth is synonymous with Asherah, the Bride of God. Her sacred grove – the famous cedars of Lebanon – were cut down to build Solomon's temple. There were 72 cedars, 72 posts in the temple, 72 spirits of the Goetia, 72 names of God. The cedars were living sacrifices. Her trees bled for JHVH. Asherah was bound first and forever.

The following is a mixture of information coming from Astaroth and others of the Legion:

The spirits of the Legion are of many sorts. Some are truly what we would call demons. Most are something else, though. They are Gods (Bael, Astaroth, Sitri, etc), deceased human spirits (Samigina, Paimon, etc.), inter-dimensional beings (Purson, Oriax), djinn, and more. It's as if Solomon took the nearest 72 convenient spirits – including the spirit of one of his most beloved wives – and bound them into this grouping in order to accomplish his great work.

As a group, they seem to prefer to be called the "Legion," as opposed to the "Goetia." Only once has our primary guide used the latter term. We asked if we might call up each spirit in turn, and she quickly said NO! "We are the Howling, and to work with us all is to invite madness." Every other time any spirit has referred to the larger group, they have always said "Legion." Moreover, Astaroth called herself the "Mother of the Legion."

Our primary guide has informed us that the distinctions of "King" or "Marquis" or "Duke" and the corresponding metals that are associated with them mean nothing to the spirits. That information, incidentally, was an editorial addition by Crowley which showed the spirits supposed planetary alignments. The spirits themselves don't agree with these associations, per se, and they respond no better to their sigils engraved in their purported planetary metal than they do to their sigils printed or drawn onto paper.

Each spirit rules over a certain number of lesser spirits – egregores or familiars or spirit guides. When these lesser spirits have gained enough strength and power (usually through helping people), they become more like their captains within the Legion. When the "captains" (the 72 named spirits) gain enough power, they become Gods. They have more freedom and strength, but they will remain bound to the Legion unless the entire body is unleashed (and forgotten).

While a great many spirits listed in the ranks of the Legion are helpful, others are ambivalent, a few are mischievous, and a handful are servants of the Adversary. These few true demons (these soul eaters, torturers, and murderers of mankind) were included in the Legion very intentionally. The good and the bad are bound together into one unit – Legion – so that Masters afraid of the wickedness of the evil spirits wouldn't try to unbind the good.

The spirits are also bound together in the minds of magicians, which binds them together as a unit. As long as we think of them as a group, they will remain a group. Since we can't un-think a thing, they will be bound until humanity forgets about them entirely.

The ranks of the Legion are populated by untold thousands of spirits who follow ("serve") one of the 72 "captains." These lesser spirits are of a similar nature to their captains, and often the captains assign one of these others as a Witch's familiar or a person's guide.

On the Creation of the Seals

The spirits' seals are somewhat flexible in regards to their form. This is why a few spirits have more than one seal. These sigils are very much like hieroglyphs or veves, and those who feel drawn to adapting a seal should look to these similar systems of glyphs for inspiration.

Coded into the seals are specific symbol sets that can help magicians better understand the 72 spirits of the Legion. Below is a listing of the most common symbols and their meanings as used within these seals. These should act as guidelines when creating new seals:

Three dots means a very old spirit, and there are only two among the Legion who bear that mark (Astaroth and Naberius).

Little circles show realms of influence.

Crosses show good communication. (This includes all lines that cross at right angles, not just Maltese crosses.)

Moons show vision power and wisdom.

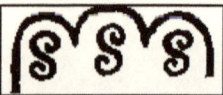

Squiggly S lines have to do with the creation of the

spirit itself (ie, used in the creation of the egregore).

 Triangles indicate crowns (high honor and power within the Legion).

The names usually written around the traditional seals are not required, but they help the master with focus and keeping all 72 spirits straight.

Careful consideration of each seal in relation to its owner's description will reveal a good deal about the seal's shape and the spirit's nature.

This book contains alternative seals which can serve as a means for inspiration in creating your own sigils for your familiar.

You may note that we have not created alternate sigils for the spirits on the DO NOT CALL list. This is a deliberate omission, as we didn't want to work directly with these spirits in order to fashion new and clearer symbols. For us, that would involve evoking those spirits in order to better understand and represent them.

On Solomon's Ring and Being Chosen of Jehovah

Some readers of this text will undoubtedly compare our descriptions of the spirits with older versions of the *Goetia*. In some places, we will make reference to these translations, as well.

One notable omission will occur in the case of several spirits. The older texts will say something like, "The exorcist must hold the magic ring to his face." This comes up especially in the case of spirits on the DO NOT CALL list. These older versions also include a description of the magic ring (or possibly disc) and how to make it.

This ring (which is sometimes described as a silver or gold ring worn on the middle finger of the left hand, and is sometimes described as a silver or gold disc inscribed with three names) is supposed to be a protection against the foul and flaming breath of these most evil demons. It is also intended to compel them into speaking the truth.

Our primary guide from the Legion, however, has informed us that such a ring was a special dispensation to Solomon. He was chosen of JHVH, who had a spirit instruct him in the correct manufacture of the ring for himself. It was a personal tool, and it won't protect anyone but Solomon from Beleth, Asmoday, or the others.

Indeed, the only way to protect yourself is not to call on spirits whose aim it is to harm you. Even then, I might add, that we and our covenmates have had to take special precautions against some of these spirits. We never called forth any of the spirits on the DO NOT CALL list, but the fact that such a list is included in this book made us targets for psychic attack by a few of the nastier demons. They primarily invaded our dreams and caused great psychic and emotional pain until we consciously protected ourselves with our most trusted talismans. The attacks could have been worse, and perhaps unstoppable, if we had directly called them into our space.

On the Greater Legion

Of the surprising pieces of information Natalie and I gleaned while discussing the 72 spirits of the Legion with our familiars, one of the most surprising had to be that there are more than 72 spirits in the Legion.

We haven't delved into this too deeply yet because the current work was large enough without doubling it. To explore 72 (or more) undocumented spirits seems daunting, though it is a task that we will be undertaking soon.

Here's what we do know:

The 72 spirits of the Legion (the ones listed in THIS book, who are sometimes collectively called the Shemhamphorash) were bound together as a unit for a specific magical working. Under their command are many thousands of lesser spirits.

However, other spirits have been created and bound into working "Legions" from one or more separate magical workings. (Some of these spirits in the Second and Third Legions are those "lesser spirits" from the Shemhamphorash, having grown in power enough to become "captains" of their own.)

However they may have come to exist, there is more than one Legion of daemons who are available for spirit conjuration. Many of the names of these other spirits are known to us via history and lore, while others have worked anonymously over the centuries – or haven't worked at all.

Demonic DO NOT CALL List

This is a list of spirits that you shouldn't summon. This is not an arbitrary list, nor is it based on personal, human opinion. Our guides within the Legion suggested this list and pointed out specific names for inclusion.

You'll note that there are some questionable, if not outright nasty, spirits whose names aren't on this list. Only those who serve the Adversary are listed here. These spirits, if called into your magical space, will lie to you, devise ways to deliver your soul to torture, kill you, or hurt those whom you love. They serve themselves and Oblivion; but they will never serve you, no matter how great your Will nor how much they feign obeisance.

To call these is to admit defeat. To call these is to ask to join their service.

7 Amon

13 Bileth

17 Botis

23 Aim

25 Glasia-Labolas

32 Asmoday

63 Andras

68 Belial

Correspondences

Creating a usable Table of Correspondences is no easy task where the Legion is concerned. As we have been told by several spirits within the Legion, not all spirits have a sign, planet, element, or direction with which they are associated. Most have at least one of these associations, and a rare few have all of them. However, to create a table in which every cell is full would require force, and it would ultimately be inauthentic for the contemporary Witch.

The information that follows is partially taken from the original texts and partially derived from our talking board and pendulum conversations with our guides. Take the following information, then, for what you will. It is meant to help you find the spirits who can best assist you. It is not meant to be a definitive compendium. Feel free to dig deeper and seek out your own associations and understandings.

Furthermore, we are informed that the tables in Crowley's *Liber 777* (which associate the spirits of the Legion with astrological decans – and, by extension, with the classical planets, elements, directions, Tarot cards, metals, incenses, and more) can be useful to the Mage who feels inclined toward that system. There is an egregore surrounding that system that has gathered energy since at least the time of its first publishing in 1909. (Since it was extrapolated and revised from an earlier Golden Dawn text, the egregore has been living and working within the magical community for many years prior to that, as well).

	Spirit	Sign	Planet	Element	Direction
1	Bael		Mercury		
2	Agares		Mars		
3	Vassago		Moon	Water	
4	Samigina				
5	Marbas	Leo	Mercury		
6	Valefor				
7	Amon	DO NOT CALL			
8	Barbatos	Sagittarius	Jupiter		
9	Paimon		Venus		West
10	Buer	Sagittarius			
11	Gusion				
12	Sitri	Aquarius	Venus	Water	
13	Beleth	DO NOT CALL			
14	Leraje	Sagittarius			
15	Eligos		Mars		
16	Zepar		Mars		
17	Botis				
18	Bathin		Moon		
19	Sallos		Mars		
20	Purson				
21	Marax	Taurus			
22	Ipos	Leo			
23	Aim	DO NOT CALL			
24	Nebarius				
25	Glasya-Labolas	DO NOT CALL			

	Spirit	Sign	Planet	Element	Direction
26	Bune		Saturn		
27	Ronove				
28	Berith	Aries			
29	Astaroth	Virgo	Venus		West
		Libra			
30	Forneus			Water	
31	Foras			Water	
32	Asmoday	DO NOT CALL			
33	Gaap	Scorpio			South
		Leo			
		Taurus			
		Aquarius			
34	Furfur			Fire	
35	Marchosias				
36	Stolas				
37	Phenex	Leo	Sun	Fire	
		Scorpio			
38	Halphas		Mars		
39	Malphas		Mars		
40	Raum				
41	Focalor			Water	
42	Vepar	Libra	Venus	Water	West
43	Sabnock	Aries	Mars		
		Leo			
44	Shax		Venus		
45	Vine	Gemini			
46	Bifrons	Gemini			

	Spirit	Sign	Planet	Element	Direction
47	Uvall			Air	
48	Haagenti				
49	Crocell	Cancer	Saturn	Water	
50	Furcas				
51	Balam				
52	Alloces	Leo	Mars	Fire	
53	Camio		Jupiter	Air	
54	Murmur		Moon	Water	
55	Orabos				
56	Gremory	Cancer	Venus	Water	
57	Ose		Mercury		East
58	Amy			Fire	
59	Oriax	Leo			
60	Vapula	Cancer Virgo Libra Pisces	Venus	Water	
61	Zagan				
62	Valak			Earth	
63	Andras	DO NOT CALL			
64	Haures		Sun	Fire	East
65	Andrealphus				
66	Kamaris				South
67	Amdusias				
68	Belial	DO NOT CALL			
69	Decarabia	Virgo Capricorn	Venus	Water	East

	Spirit	Sign	Planet	Element	Direction
70	Seere				
71	Dantalion				
72	Andromalius	Libra			

Areas of Influence and Interest

The following quick reference is intended to help you find those spirits who are skilled in the areas in which you need assistance or have an interest. Please do not rely solely on this list, but instead use it as a way to narrow the field. The spirit descriptions that follow will be much more informative regarding the specific manner in which each spirit can help you with the topics and skills listed below.

Alchemy, Transmutation, Transformation	5 – Marbas
	48 – Haagenti
	59 – Oriax
	61 – Zagan
Animal Communication	8 – Barbatos
	53 – Camio
	69 – Decarabia
Astral Travel, Spirit Journeying	33 – Gaap
Astronomy, Astrology, Star Lore	21 – Marax
	36 – Stolas
	50 – Furcas
	52 – Alloces
	58 – Amy
	59 – Oriax
	65 – Andrealphus
Athletics	2 – Agares
Competition	14 – Leraje

Destruction	40 – Raum
	41 – Focalor
	43 – Sabnock
	64 – Haures
Discord	17 – Botis
Disease, Wounds (cause)	42 – Vepar
	43 – Sabnock
	64 – Haures
Divination, Scrying, Visions	3 – Vassago
	5 – Marbas
	8 – Barbatos
	9 – Paimon
	11 – Gusion
	15 – Eligos
	17 – Botis
	20 – Purson
	21 – Marax
	22 – Ipos
	26 – Bune
	28 – Berith
	29 – Astaroth
	30 – Forneus
	33 – Gaap
	34 – Furfur
	40 – Raum
	45 – Vine
	47 – Uvall
	53 – Camio
	54 – Murmur

	56 – Gremory
	57 – Ose
	64 – Haures
	69 – Decarabia
Energy Movement	62 – Valak
Friendship, Alliances	47 – Uvall
	55 – Orabos
Geometry (and all math)	46 – Bifrons
	49 – Crocell
	65 – Andrealphus
Good Familiars	6 – Valefor
	10 – Buer
	20 – Purson
	21 – Marax
	27 – Ronove
	36 – Stolas
	43 – Sabnock
	44 – Shax
	51 – Alloces
	67 – Amdusias
Languages	2 – Agares
	27 – Ronove
Law, Ethics, Justice	24 – Nebarius
	53 – Camio
	72 – Andromalius
Liberal Arts (all)	9 – Paimon
	24 – Nebarius
	29 – Astaroth

	46 – Bifrons
	71 – Dantalion
Liberal Sciences (all)	4 – Samigina
	9 – Paimon
	21 – Marax
	24 – Nebarius
	29 – Astaroth
	33 – Gaap
	37 – Phenex
	46 – Bifrons
	49 – Crocell
	50 – Furcas
	51 – Balam
	52 – Alloces
	57 – Ose
	58 – Amy
	60 – Vapula
	71 – Dantalion
Logic	10 – Buer
	31 – Foras
	50 – Furcas
	66 – Kamaris
Love, Lust, Sex	9 – Paimon
	12 – Sitri
	15 – Eligos
	19 – Sallos
	34 – Furfur
	40 – Raum
	44 – Shax

	47 – Uvall
	60 – Vapula
Mechanical Arts, Building	5 – Marbas
Medicine, Healing	5 – Marbas
	10 – Buer
Money	40 – Raum
	44 – Shax
Music, Singing, Poetry	9 – Paimon
	42 – Vepar
	67 – Amdusias
Mysteries, Hidden Things, Secrets	5 – Marbas
	8 – Barbatos
	15 – Eligos
	20 – Purson
	29 – Astaroth
	30 – Forneus
	37 – Phenex
	44 – Shax
	45 – Vine
	55 – Orabos
	56 – Gremory
	64 – Haures
	66 – Kamaris
	71 – Dantalion
	72 – Andromalius
Necromancy	4 – Samigina
	26 – Bune
	46 – Bifrons
	54 – Murmur

Philosophy	10 – Buer
	33 – Gaap
	50 – Furcas
	54 – Murmur
	60 – Vapula
Properties of Herbs, Plants, Woods	8 – Barbatos
	10 – Buer
	18 – Bathin
	21 – Marax
	31 – Foras
	36 – Stolas
	46 – Bifrons
Properties of Stones	8 – Barbatos
	18 – Bathin
	21 – Marax
	31 – Foras
	36 – Stolas
	46 – Bifrons
	69 – Decarabia
Reputation, Dignity, Praise, Honors, Awards	55 – Orabos
	59 – Oriax
Rhetoric, Communication, Debate	11 – Gusion
	24 – Nebarius
	26 – Bune
	27 – Ronove
	31 – Foras
	50 – Furcas
	53 – Camio
	66 – Kamaris

Shapeshifting	1 – Bael
	57 – Ose
	65 – Andrealphus
Sleight of Hand	6 – Valefor
Speaking in Tongues	30 – Forneus
Tree Communication	8 – Barbatos
	67 – Amdusias
War, Strategy, Defense	15 – Eligos
	16 – Zepar
	19 – Sallos
	38 – Halphas
	39 – Malphas
	43 – Sabnock
Water, Sea, Sailing	41 – Focalor
	42 – Vepar
	49 – Crocell
Weather Magic	34 – Furfur
	41 – Focalor
	42 – Vepar
Witchcraft	10 – Buer
	18 – Bathin

The Spirits of the Legion

"Bael" © 2013 John Birkel

(1.) BAEL

Bael is a great magician and serves Azazel in all things. He knows much magic. The teachings of Azazel are his domain, which is why he is number 1 among the 72. He is said to make the Master to go invisible. This is because he has mastery over shape-shifting and masking. Make-up is a form of masking.

He appears in many shapes, sometimes like a cat, sometimes like a toad, sometimes like a man; and he sometimes all these forms at once. He is ugly but strong. He has horns upon his head. He speaks hoarsely.

Bael is old. He is Baal, Bel, Beltane Azazel.

Traditional Sigil

Alternate Sigil

"Bael" © *2013 Natalie Black*

(2.) AGARES

He serves Ares. Agares (pronounced Aj-aries) is an athlete. Classic descriptions of Agares show him "riding upon a crocodile, carrying a goshawk upon his fist, and yet mild in appearance." In this case, the crocodile is a symbol for Typhon. He has the power to ground chaos. The bird is a symbol for sport. However, he doesn't actually appear before the Master with these animals. He just comes as a person. He's not ugly. He looks as a fighter would look in his prime.

He helps people develop their athletic abilities, and he is a master of all feats of physical prowess. He is reported to bring back runaways, but this was a reference to runaway slaves. If you need to bring home a runaway child, pet, or lover, there are better spirits for that task.

He teaches all languages or tongues quickly. He helps you if you're trying to learn a new language. (There are spirits that help you speak in tongues, but Agares isn't one of them.)

Very physical is Agares, hence his association with earthquakes.

Alternate Sigil

"Vassago" © 2013 Natalie Black

(3.) VASSAGO

The third spirit is Vassago. This spirit is of a good nature, and his office is to declare things past and to come and to discover all things hidden or lost. He can see deep into time and is great at scrying. He works via visions. He rarely talks. He is for those who "see." However, he has many friends in the Legion, if the Master wishes him to work in conjunction with other spirits who do speak.

The moons in his seal show his vision power.

He looks like a man with big eyes and glasses.

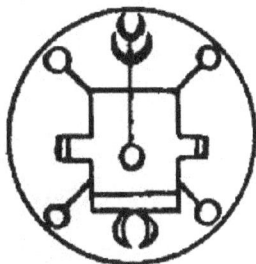

Traditional Sigil   *Alternate Sigil*

"Samigina" © 2013 John Birkel

(4.) SAMIGINA

Samigina (pronounced Somma-jenna, "like a whisper") appears to the Master like a "Dark Alice" – a young woman with long, dark blonde hair. (She prefers simply to be called "S," and is known thusly within the Enochian angelic tablets.)

Her preferred animal form is that of a little horse, which is symbolic of her carrying the Dead.

She teaches all liberal sciences, and gives account of *all* dead souls (some sources say "who died at sea," which is symbolic of the Underworld or Land of the Dead). She can do a bit of anything, but her special talent is with the Dead.

She is *very* communicative. She is a *ghede* among the Voudon loa, and indeed her seal is nearly identical to Baron Samhedi's veve.

Traditional Sigil

Alternate Sigil

"Samigina" © 2013 Natalie Black

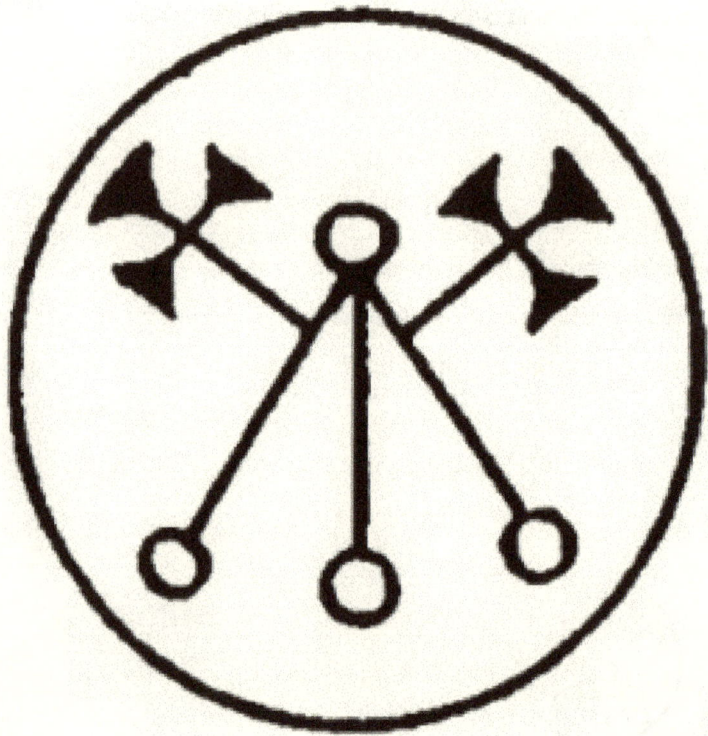

(5.) MARBAS

He appears at first in the form of a large lion, but afterwards, at the request of the Master, he puts on human shape. In fact, he prefers to look like John Dee, for his own reasons.

He answers truly of things hidden or secret. He is communicative.

He causes diseases and cures them. He is the Legion's alchemist. He is friendly and wise. Marbas is more of a pharmacist than healer.

He gives great wisdom and knowledge in mechanical arts. He can use chemistry to build. Also he has a great lab and can help others build such things – especially automobiles and combustion engines, which are a sort of modern alchemy.

His symbol is supposed to look like lab equipment, which shows that he is good at many things that stem from alchemy.

Alternate Sigil

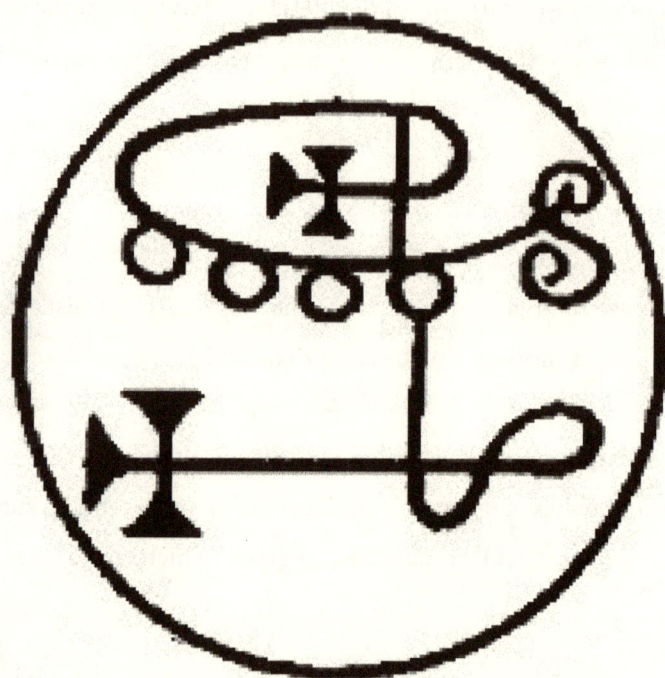

(6.) VALEFOR

Pronounced: Vail-for. He appears in the shape of a man-lion, much like the character of the Cowardly Lion from the *Wizard of Oz*.

He is a good familiar.

Older texts say that he tempts them he is a familiar of to steal; but in truth, he is a master at sleight of hand and teaches that art to his Master.

His seal shows an item being removed from a pocket or purse.

Alternate Sigil

(7.) AMON – DO NOT CALL

She is most stern. She appears as a dark-haired, angry woman who literally breathes fire. The description of her appearance given in older versions of the *Goetia* describes her exhibiting fearsome features (wolf with a serpent's tail, a raven's head, and dog's teeth), but these are all symbolic of her fierceness. Our guide assures us that she does sometimes have a raven's head, however, and she breathes fire. She is frightening to behold.

She is an instigator of gossip. She can end feuds, but she prefers to start them.

Her sigil is an open mouth, ready to devour (or shouting lies).

(8.) BARBATOS

The old texts say that "he appears when the Sun is in Sagittarius, with four noble kings and their companies of great troops." The kings are metaphors for Jesus and the three wise men, and the company of great troops are angels. So, he often first appears to a Master in the days preceding the Winter Solstice.

He gives understanding of the singing of birds and of the voices of other creatures (such as the barking of dogs). He is the Lord of Nature. He can teach the Master to have true communication with all of nature.

He breaks the "hidden treasures open that have been laid by the enchantments of magicians." Specifically, these "hidden treasures" are metaphors for holy gifts, the spiritual gifts of clairvoyance, clairaudience, hands-on healing, etc.

He is very holy. He is a servant of Jesus, and there is a saint very like him – Saint Francis!

He knows all things past and to come, and he brings friendships and leadership to the Master.

His sigil is an altar, similar to the ancient incense altars.

Alternate Sigil

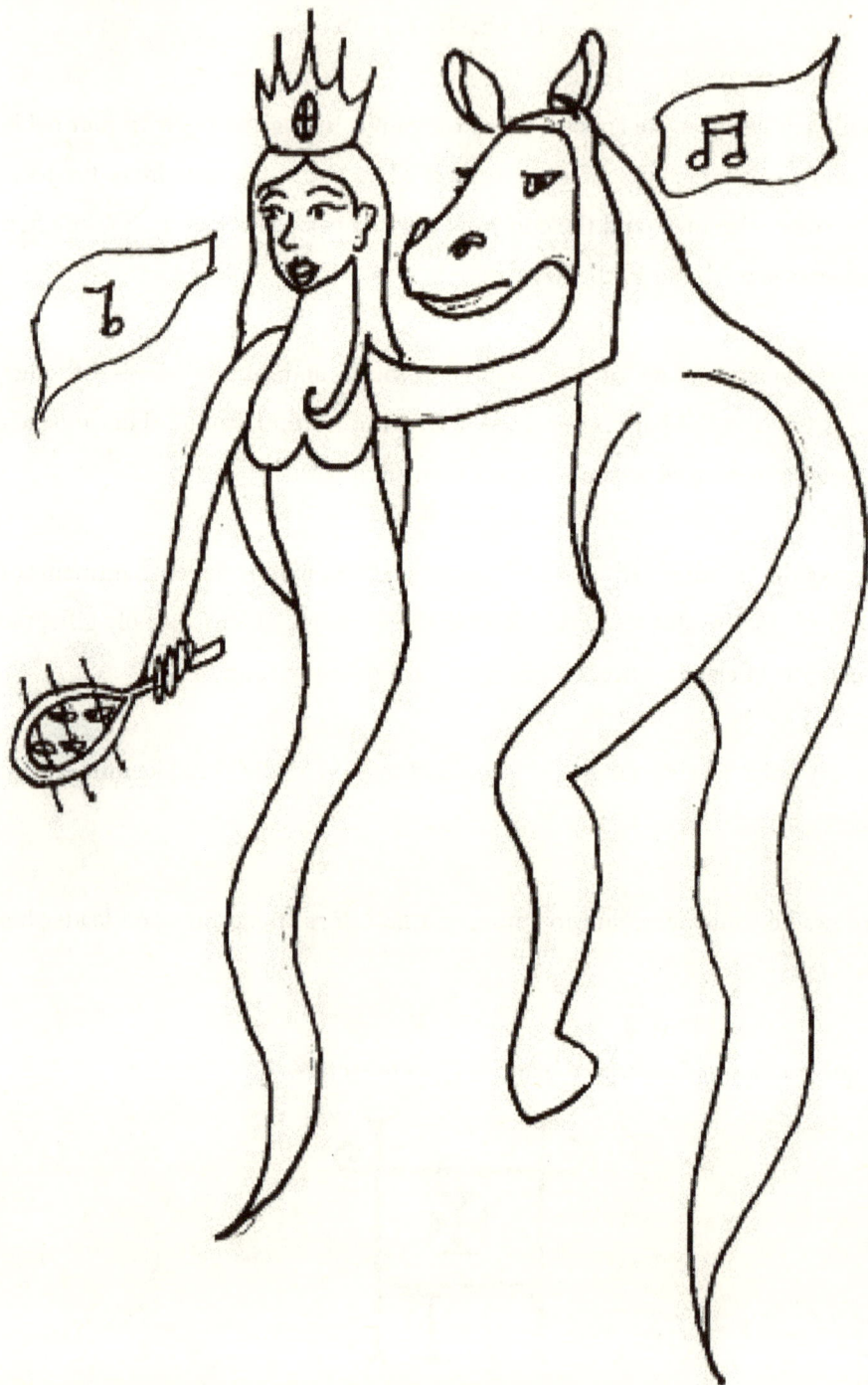

"Paimon" © 2013 Natalie Black

(9.) PAIMON

Pronounced: Pay-mon. She is a very vain and beautiful woman sitting upon a camel with a glorious crown upon her head. She appears to the Master with a full entourage (previously described as a parade complete with musicians), and she insists upon singing, which is what makes her difficult to understand to all except those with whom she has close affinity.

She can teach all arts and sciences and other secret things. She is quite clever, and she fancies herself a queen among the spirits. Indeed, she was a queen in her mortal life – the Queen of Sheba, one of Solomon's wives.

She binds or makes any man subject unto the Mage, if desired. In truth, this is her greatest magic and her special skill.

She gives good familiars and appears in the West within your sphere.

She is very nice and quite easy to work with, but she demands a great deal of attention. For instance, she wants offerings at each meeting, and she usually presents herself with two esteemed members of her entourage called LABAL and ABALI.

Paimon's sigil depicts a singing, dancing, and instrument-filled procession.

Traditional Sigil

Alternate Sigil

"Buer" © 2013 John Birkel

(10.) BUER

He is strongest when the sun is in Sagittarius, and he appears in the shape of a centaur or archer during that time.

He teaches philosophy, both moral and natural, and the art of logic. He also teaches the virtues of all herbs and plants. He heals all distempers in man, and he gives good Familiars.

He is a friendly spirit, especially to Witches.

Buer often appears in the form of a great wheel, and he is lovely to behold. His seal is meant to resemble herbs or flowers.

Alternate Sigil

(11.) GUSION

Pronounced: Goosey-own.

He appears like a chimera – many beasts, always changing. He tells all things past, present, and to come, and he shows the meaning and resolution of all questions you may ask.

He is a great communicator, and he helps the Master to communicate well.

He can be moody.

His seal looks like a gate to represent the many beasts whose shapes he assumes. He opens the gate and lets another beast free.

Alternate Sigil

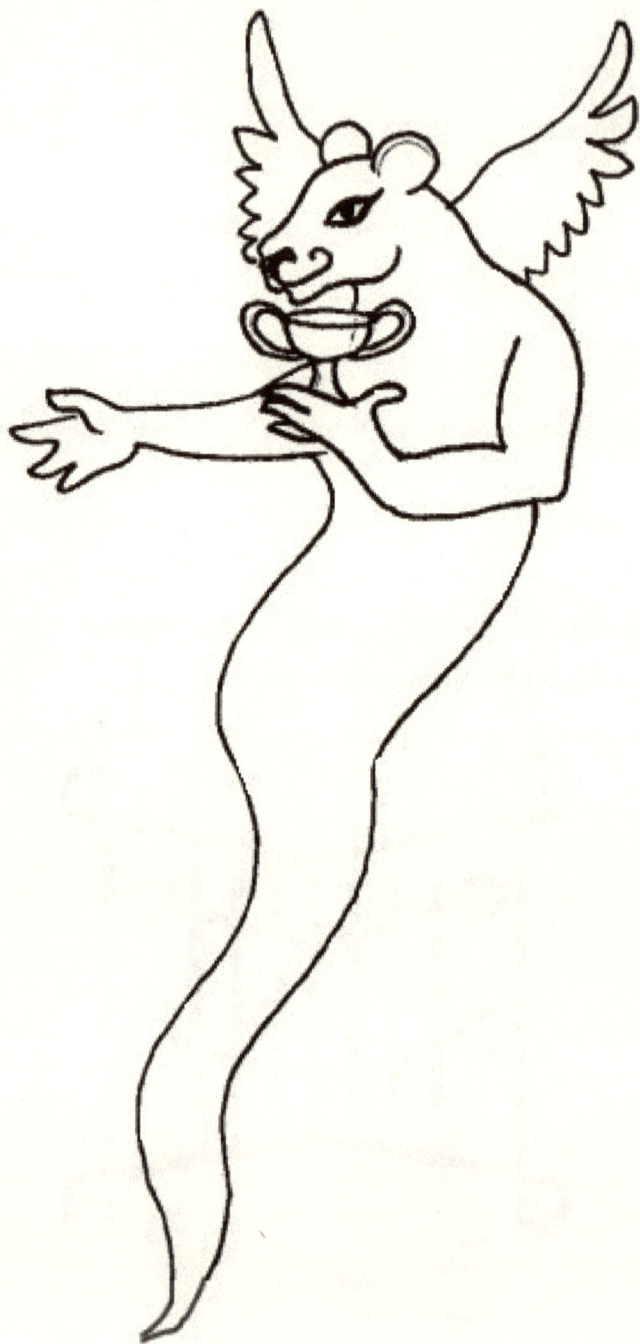

"Sitri" © 2013 Natalie Black

(12.) SITRI

He is like Cupid, and when people speak of the Angel of Love, they are speaking of Sitri.

He appears at first with a leopard's head and gryphon's wings, but the rest is human and very beautiful.

He enflames men with women's love, and women with men's love; and he causes them to show themselves naked, if that is the desire of the Master.

His sigil is the Loving Cup.

Traditional Sigil

Alternate Sigil

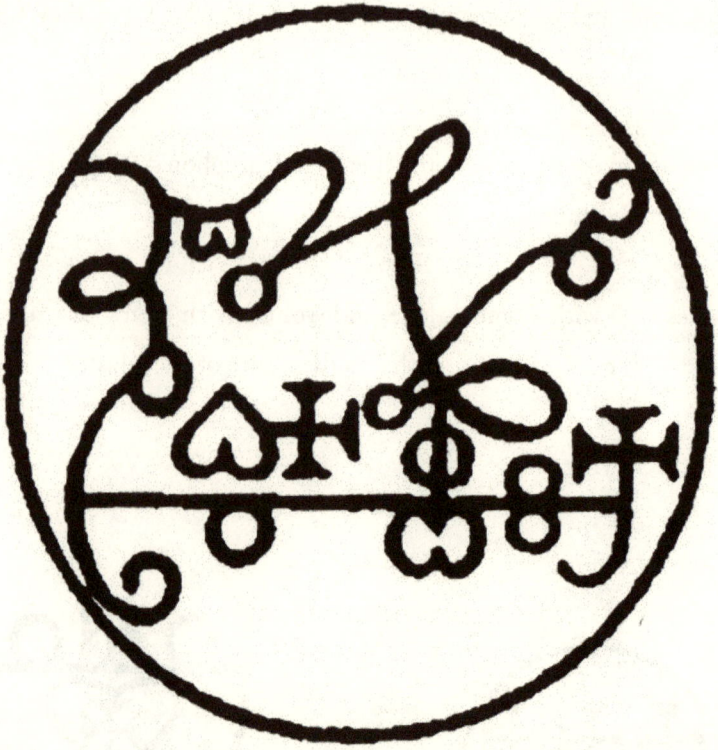

(13.) BELETH – DO NOT CALL

The thirteenth spirit is called Beleth (or Bileth, Billith, Bilet).

We are told he is a "bloodthirsty bastard."

He rides on a pale horse with trumpets and other kinds of musical instruments playing in procession before him. He is very furious.

The older texts say that a Master must hold a hazel wand in his hand, striking it out towards the South and East quarters, make a triangle without the circle, and then command him into it by the bonds and charges of spirits as are written in those texts. This is supposed to give you the ability to control Beleth and force him to tell the truth. However, this is a spirit that a Master cannot control. He helps only himself. Any agreement made is a true deal with the devil.

The texts then go onto say that putting a magic ring to your face will protect the Master from the flaming breath of the enraged spirit. We are informed, however, that this technique will not protect you from Beleth or his flaming breath.

Beleth is very strong and serves only himself; however, he can create lust in both men and women. If it is a spirit of love and lust that you seek, though, there are others better suited to the task.

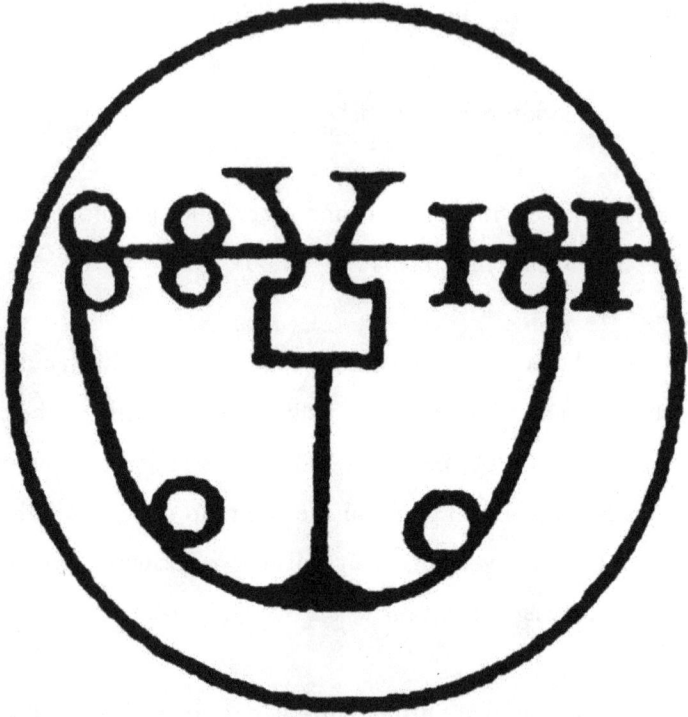

(14.) LERAJE

The fourteenth spirit is called Leraje (or Leraie or Leraikha). She does not care by which name you call her, nor the pronunciation you use.

She shows herself in the likeness of an archer clad in green with long pretty red hair, carrying a bow and quiver.

She is the lady of competition. She is a good spirit for those with Sun in Sagittarius.

She is not very talkative, much like the other spirits of action.

Her sigil looks like a bow and arrow.

Alternate Sigil

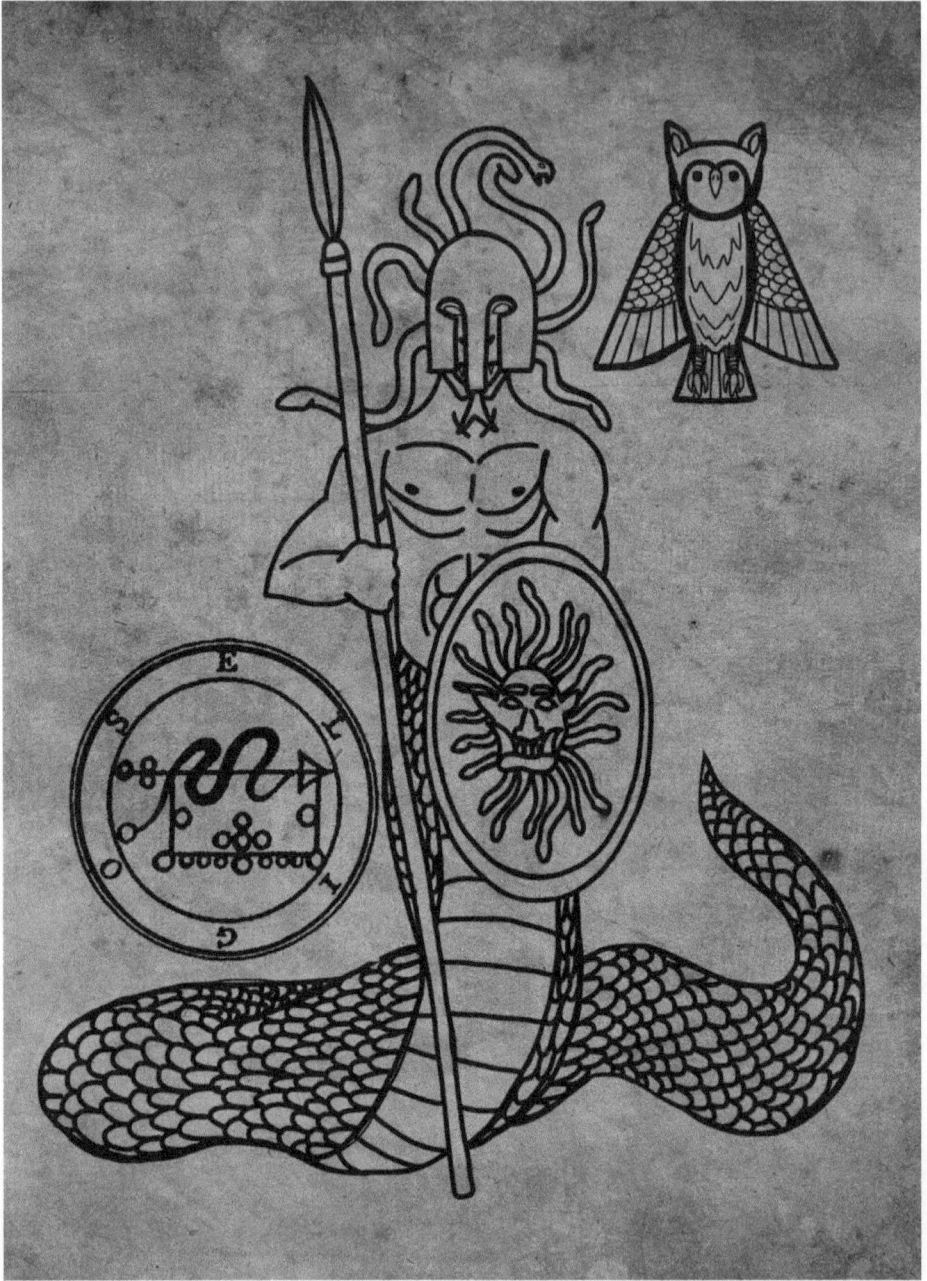

"Eligos" © 2013 John Birkel

(15.) ELIGOS

Pronounced: Elleh-goss.

He appears in the form of a snake. He is in the service of Athena, and he is her serpent. He can be thought of as Erechthonius, Athena's son by Hephaestus and the first ruler of Athens.

He discovers hidden things and knows things to come. He knows of wars and how battles will be decided. He causes love for people in political power.

His sigil looks like a serpent holding a lance.

Alternate Sigil

(16.) ZEPAR

Zepar is a soldier, and he appears in the form and uniform of a contemporary soldier.

He is very sad, for he has lost many masters young. He is often a familiar to soldiers and their wives, and he is the spirit who answers all prayers for protection for soldiers.

His sigil is a shield and weapons.

Alternate Sigil

(17.) BOTIS

He appears at first in the form of an ugly viper, then at the command of the Magician he puts on a human shape with great teeth and two horns, carrying a bright and sharp sword in his hand.

He tells all things past and to future, and he sows discord among friends and foes.

He's not a nice guy, but certainly not the worst. If all you want is to make enemies, then it is safe to work with Botis. His words are poison.

"Bathin" © 2013 Natalie Black

(18.) BATHIN

Pronounced: Bay-thin.

He appears like a strong man with the tail of a serpent, sitting upon a pale-colored steed. This pale steed is the mist of magic, and Bathin is well-aligned to Witches.

He knows the virtues of herbs and precious stones.

He has two sigils. One features a moon, depicting his wisdom (as shown below). The other features a cross, showing his strength in communication (not included in this book). Both are appropriate, and a Master could combine these images in a way that highlights both features, as we have done in our alternate sigil below.

Traditional Sigil   *Alternate Sigil*

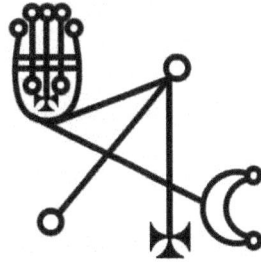

(19.) SALLOS

Sallos (or Saleos) appears in the form of a gallant soldier riding on a crocodile, with a helmet on his head.

He causes lust in both men and women. The crocodile is symbolic of base desires.

He is sort of a jerk, according to the other spirits. He is a drunk and a loud-mouth.

"Purson" © 2013 Natalie Black

(20.) PURSON

Purson's appearance is not attractive by human standards. He looks "kind of like a bear, if the bear was a [messed] up inter-dimensional bear." He has tentacles for hands. Going before him are many trumpets blaring. He can take any aërial body, like that of various alien species; but he cannot take a human body.

He knows all things hidden and can discover treasure. He can tell all things past, present, and to come. He answers truly of all earthly things both secret and divine, and of the creation of the world.

He is very strong and friendly, and he gives good familiars. He leads many spirits, "but they are all xeno" (alien).

His seal is meant to look like a strange bear with tentacles.

Traditional Sigil

Alternate Sigil

"Marax" © 2013 John Birkel

(21.) MARAX

He appears like a man with a bull's face, similar to a Minotaur.

His office is to make men very knowledgeable in astronomy and all other liberal sciences; also he can give good, wise familiars, knowledgeable in the properties and uses of herbs and gems.

He is particularly helpful for those with the sign of Taurus.

He doesn't speak much. He usually has familiars speak for him.

His sigil is meant to represent the sign of Taurus.

Alternate Sigil

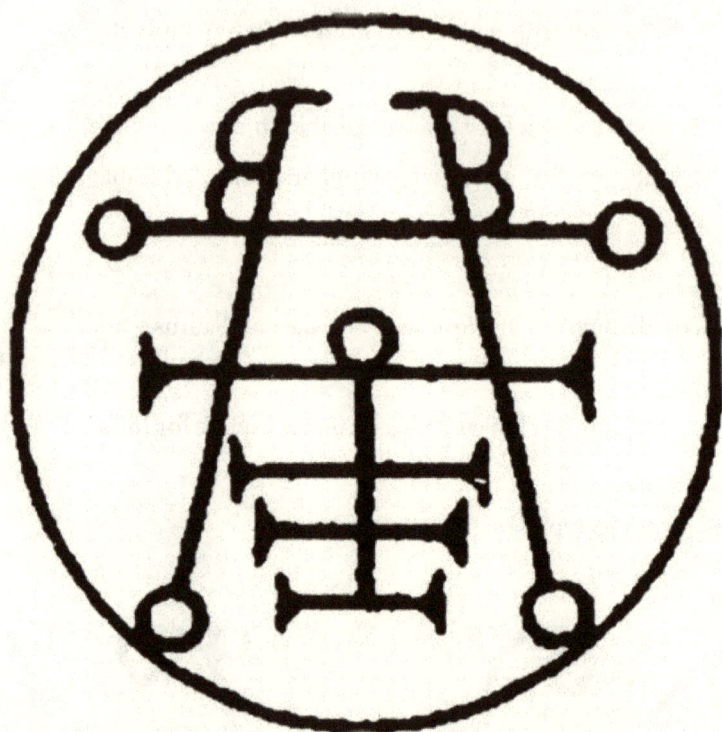

(22.) IPOS

Pronounced: Eep-ose.

He appears in the form of an angel with both a lion's head and a human's head, goose wings, and a hare's tail. Sometimes the human face is male, at other times it is female. He looks like an angel, but he is not one.

He knows all things past, present, and to come.

He makes men witty and bold, as he himself is. He is very reckless and fast. He is friendly enough, but he is tricky.

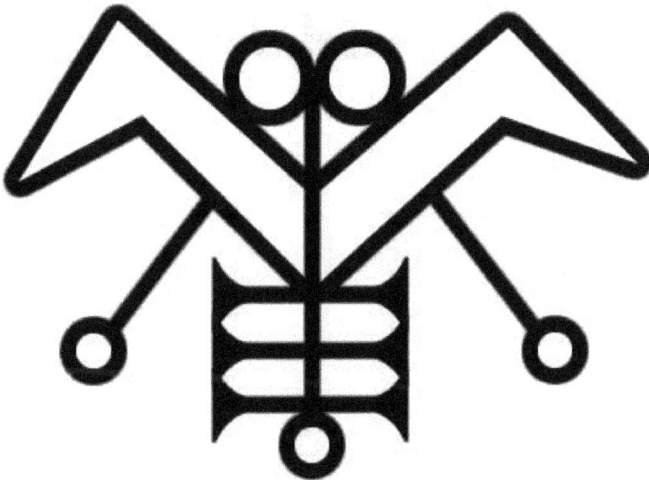

Alternate Sigil

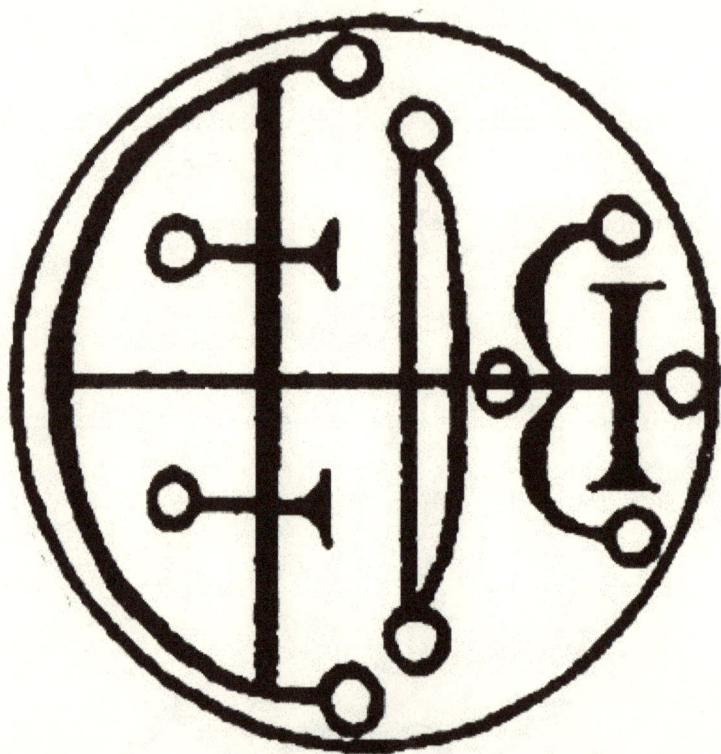

(23.) AIM – DO NOT CALL

Aim appears in the form of a very handsome man in body, but with many heads. One is like a serpent, another like a man having two stars on his forehead, a third like a calf. He may appear with other heads, as well, sometimes showing multiple faces at the same time.

He carries a fiery sword in his hand, with which he sets cities, castles, and great places on fire.

He is insane.

He *can* give true answers unto private matters, but he is not to be trusted. He lies and enjoys destruction, mayhem, and madness.

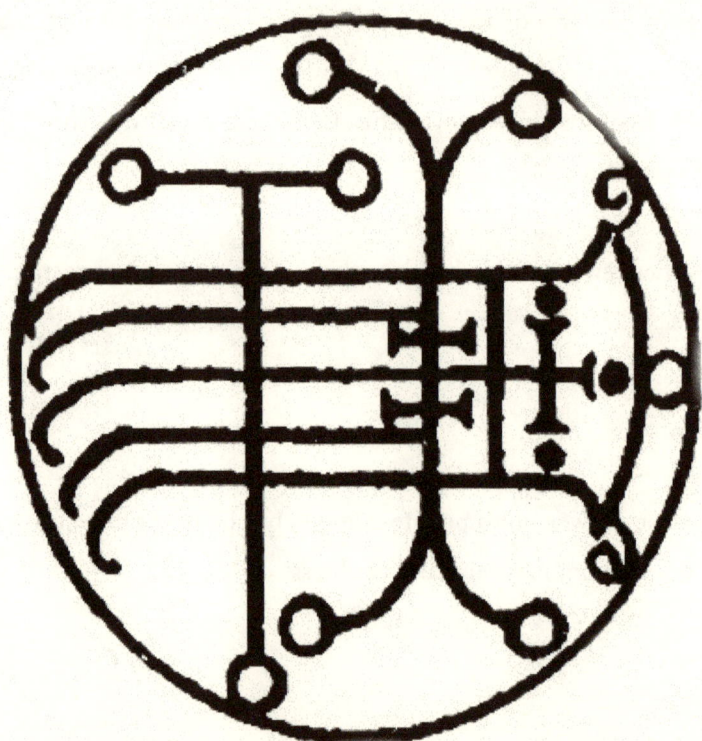

(24.) NABERIUS

Naberius is a most valiant spirit, showing himself in the form of a black crane fluttering about the circle. He often looks like a black Thoth in a black suit. He speaks eloquently and clearly.

He is cunning in all arts and sciences, but especially in the art of rhetoric. He is especially knowledgeable in the areas of law and ethics, and he can use these to trick the Master, if he chooses.

Alternate Sigil

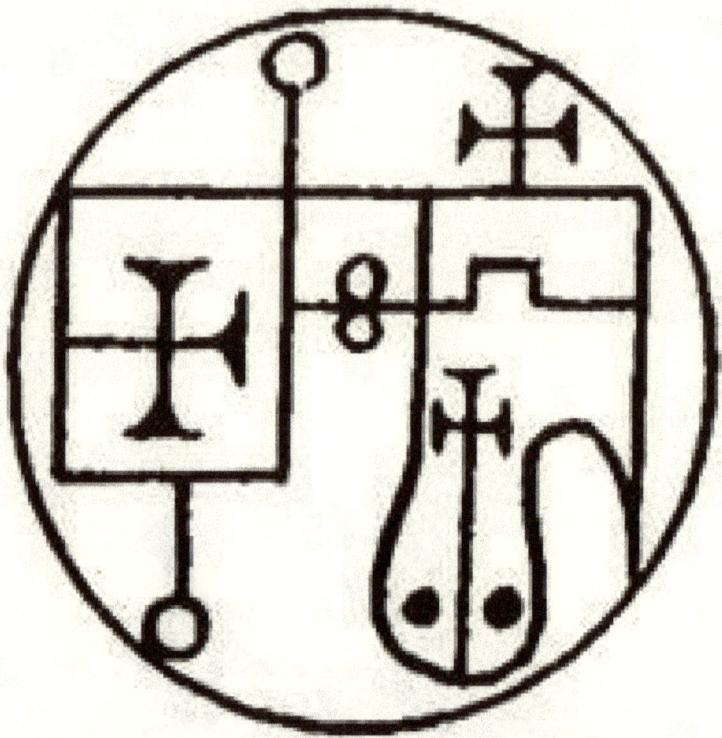

(25.) GLASYA-LABOLAS – DO NOT CALL

He shows himself in the form of a dog with wings like a gryphon.

He is an author of bloodshed and manslaughter. He will lead the Master on, making you believe you are in control of the situation or even dealing with a spirit who cares for you, until such time as he can devise your accidental death.

He is very talkative and convincing.

"Bune" © 2013 John Birkel

(26.) BUNE

Bune (or Bime) is a strong and caring spirit, appearing in the form of a three-headed dragon. He speaks with a high and lovely voice. He is a spirit of necromancy and ancestor work, assisting the Master in conjuring the Dead and seeking answers from them.

He gives riches unto the Master and makes him wise and eloquent. He gives true answers unto questions.

He has two seals (one included in the illustration to the left, the other depicted below), both of which are useful. They are both meant to represent a dragon.

Traditional Sigil

Alternate Sigil

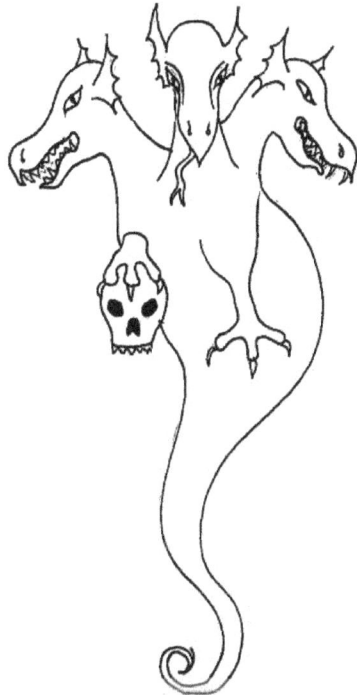

"Bune" © 2013 Natalie Black

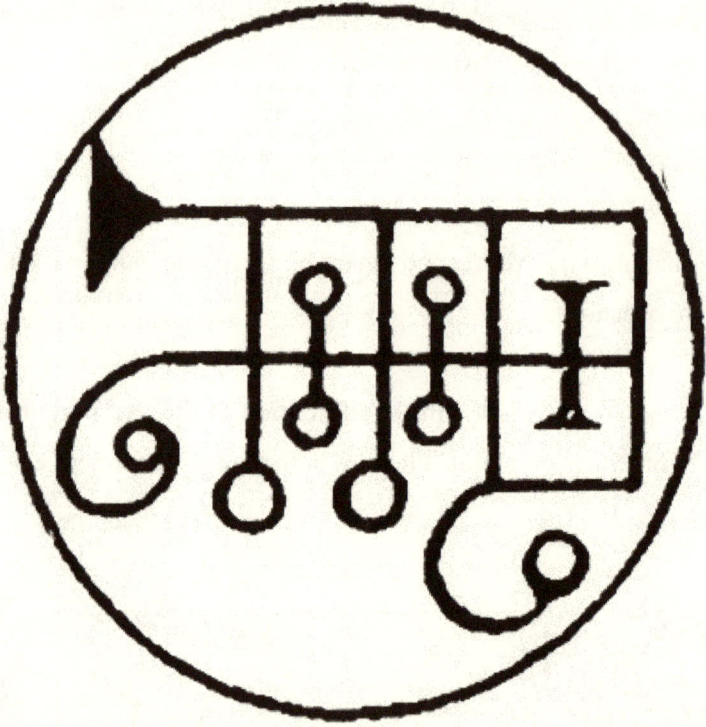

(27.) RONOVE

He appears in the form of a goblin, with a temper to match. He is not a negative or baneful spirit. He means well, but he is quite cranky.

He teaches the art of rhetoric very well and gives good familiars.

He also bestows knowledge of languages.

Ronove's sigil looks like a trumpet or megaphone.

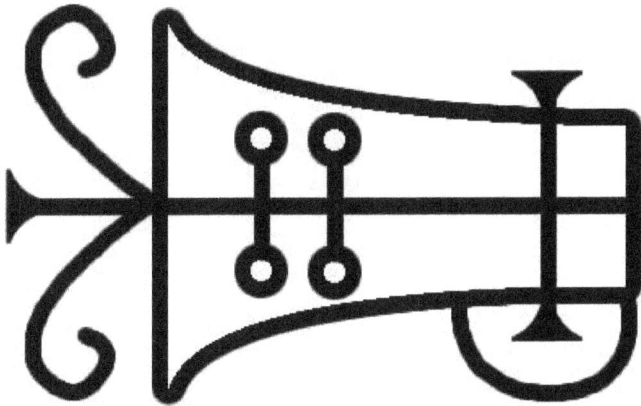

Alternate Sigil

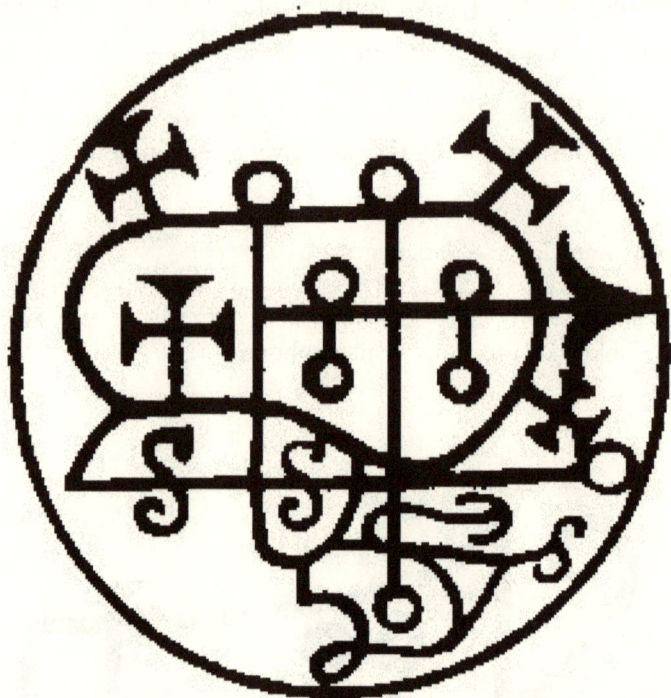

(28.) BERITH

Berith has two other names given to him by men of later times (viz.: BEALE and BOFRY).

He appears in the form of the god Mars (though he is not that deity), like a soldier with red clothing, riding upon a red horse, and having a crown of gold upon his head.

He is favorable to those born in the sign of Aries.

He can give true answers of the past and future, but he is a great liar and may not share the truth unless it suits him. He speaks with a very clear and soft voice.

Alternate Sigil

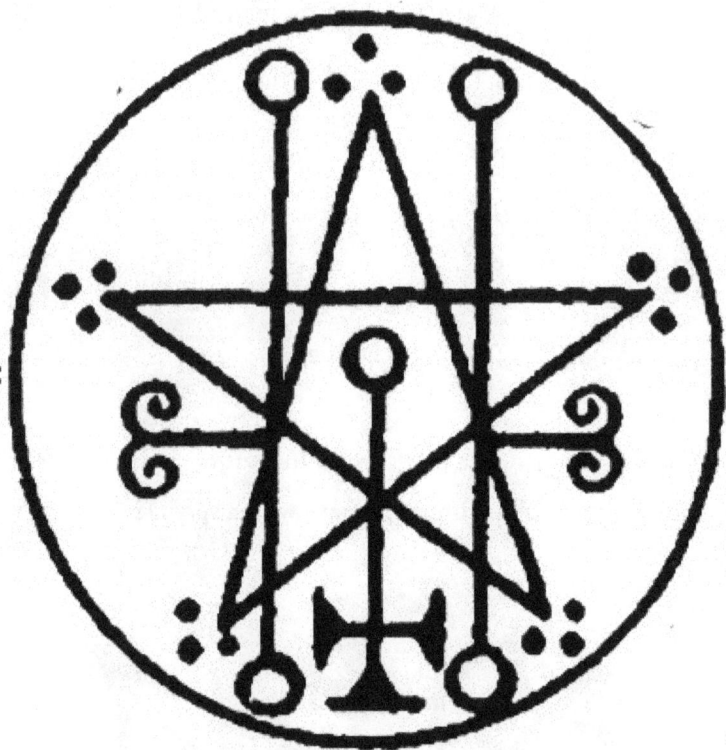

(29.) ASTAROTH

Astaroth is a Queen within the Legion, the closest that the spirits have to royalty. She is called the "Mother of the Legion" by them.

She appears as a beautiful angel carrying serpents, much like the Neolithic bird and serpent Goddesses.

You must not command her, for she is furious and dangerous in the presence of haughty and presumptuous Masters. If you call her politely, though, she is gracious and regal. Call her as you would any Goddess, for this is what she is. She is Asherah. She is Astarte. She is Ishtar.

You will know her by her breath. It is of roses for those who love her, but it is of sulfur for the unjust.

She gives true answers of things past, present, and to come, and she can discover all secrets. She will give a true and full account of the creation of the Legion. She can make men knowledgeable in all arts, sciences, and mysteries.

"Forneus" © 2013 Natalie Black

(30.) FORNEUS

She is a great sea-monster.

She is of the deep waters, and she can help you access all the information and emotion that lie hidden deep within the mind.

The art and magic she teaches is glossolalia, speaking in tongues. She is sometimes mistaken for Wisdom/Sophia, the Holy Spirit, because she teaches this art and brings hidden knowledge to the surface.

Traditional Sigil

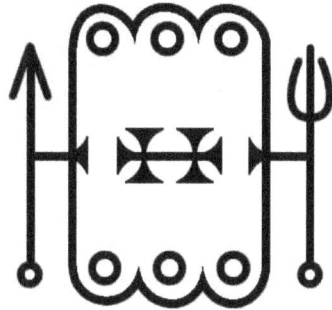

Alternate Sigil

(31.) FORAS

Foras appears in the form of a strong and virile human man.

He teaches the properties of all herbs and precious stones. He teaches the arts of logic and ethics in all their parts. He can help the Master to live long and to be eloquent.

He can discover treasures and recover lost objects.

He is very communicative, and he seems to prefer working with gay and bisexual men.

The seal of Foras is a man with lovely, long hair

Alternate Sigil

"Asmoday" © 2013 John Birkel

(32.) ASMODAY – DO NOT CALL

Asmoday (or Asmodeus) is strong and powerful. He appears with three heads – a man, a bull, and a ram. (The bull and ram show associations with the signs of Taurus and Aries. His area of influence is in the areas associated with these two signs.) He usually only appears with the head of a man when called into the pyramid.

He also has the tail of a serpent and webbed goose-feet, as is common among the spirits who are "demons" in the sense we have come to know them contemporarily. These demon-spirits are the evils of the world that seek to become Gods. Asmoday breathes fire and carries a lance with a banner.

He is bound to the Adversary and is one of his chief demons. The original texts claim that by removing your hat and asking his name, Asmoday will bow down before you and speak the truth. This is not the case. He will mock you for such silliness, and he will proceed to do as he likes.

He *can* provide the true magic ring, the Ring of Virtues; but he isn't likely to do so. He teaches arithmetic, astronomy, geometry, and all handicrafts. He gives true and full answers to your questions. He makes one invincible. He shows the place where treasures lie, and he guards it.

Asmoday is on the DO NOT CALL list, despite the many benefits one might receive in working with him, because his primary interest is in gathering human souls. We are told from within the Legion that he does this in order to feed the demons under his command. He serves a Master well in life, but he claims the Master's soul in death through bargains they have made with each other.

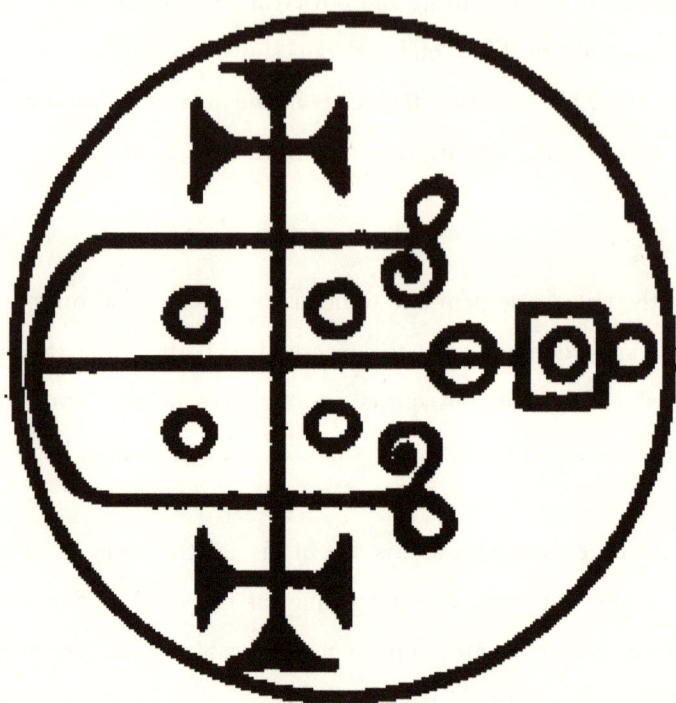

(33.) GAAP

Pronounced: Gop.

He rules the fixed signs (Leo, Scorpio, Aquarius, and Taurus), and acts as a guide to those born during these times. He makes men feel insensible or ignorant; and he can also make them feel very knowledgeable in the areas of philosophy and the liberal sciences.

He can teach you to consecrate those tools and relics that belong to the Adversary.

He can steal familiars away from other Magicians, if you demand it; but the other Magicians only need to ask him to return their familiars in order to be restored. In order to accomplish this theft, though, you must know the name of the familiar.

He answers truly and perfectly of things past, present, and to come. He also assists with astral travel.

His sigil shows him leading the four fixed signs of the zodiac.

Alternate Sigil

"Furfur" © 2013 John Birkel

(34.) FURFUR

Furfur's preferred form is that of a large, flying stag with a fiery tail. He won't speak truth unless you insist, but this is more a mark of his silliness than deceitfulness. By calling him into the pyramid, though, he will speak truth from the start. He speaks in a high, laughing voice.

He can urge love between a man and woman, using humor and wit as his tools. His greatest power, though, is in raising great storms and lightening. He teaches the Master weather magic, though he says the Mage must have horns (a headdress or loose antlers/horns) to use as a tool to accomplish this magic.

He gives true answers of divine and secret things to a Master with whom he has an affinity. He prefers those who have an outrageous sense of humor, like him.

His sigil is a deer with antlers.

Traditional Sigil

Alternate Sigil

"Furfur" © 2013 Natalie Black

(35.) MARCHOSIAS

Marchosias comes in the form of a dazed ox with gryphon's wings, belching and dribbling fire from his mouth.

He is a strong fighter and worker, but he was abused terribly during the building of the Temple. His mind is shattered. He is sweet and strong, and he believes that if he is loyal and productive he will be released from the Legion to return to the worship of the All.

Marchosias was a spirit of sacrifice – the power of the blood spilled in sacrificial rites.

His sigil is the Temple itself (the altar with the veils drawn back).

Alternate Sigil

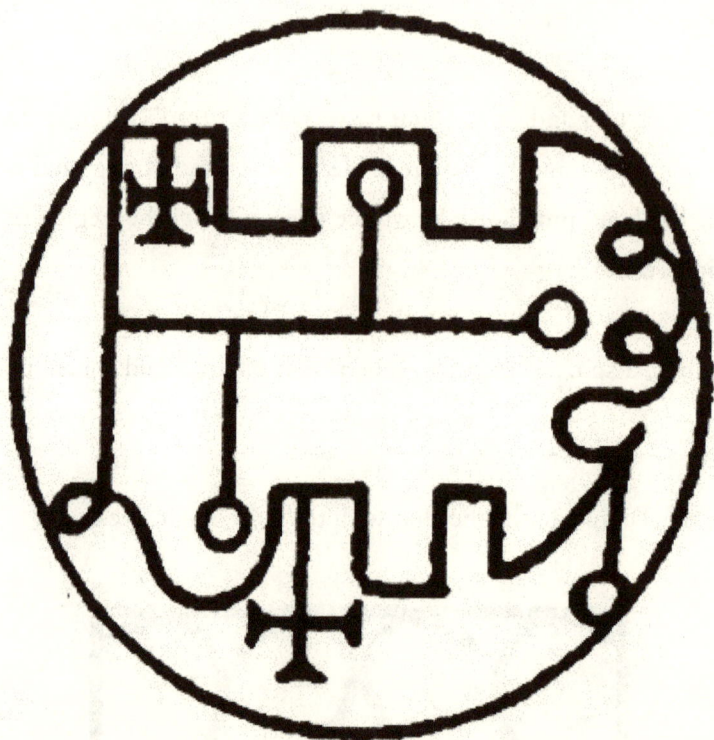

(36.) STOLAS

Stolas appears in the shape of a mighty raven.

He teaches the art of astronomy and the properties of herbs and precious stones. He makes an excellent familiar.

His sigil represents a raven's wing.

Alternate Sigil

"Phenex" © 2013 John Birkel

(37.) PHENEX

Phenex (Phoenix) appears like the bird of the same name, and speaks with the voice of a child. He sings many sweet notes upon being summoned, which can be heard by the Witch without harm. Then he will speak eloquently of wonders and science.

He is an excellent poet. And he will be willing to perform your requests.

He, like Marchosias, expects to return to singular focus on the All. Phenex is child-like and simply does not understand his situation. He is hopeful and pure.

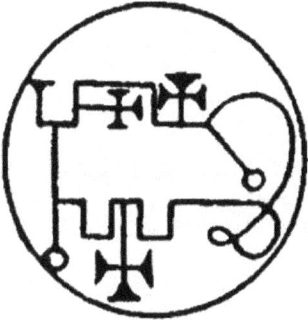

Traditional Sigil

Alternate Sigil

"Halphas & Malphas" © 2013 Natalie Black

Traditional Seal of Halphas

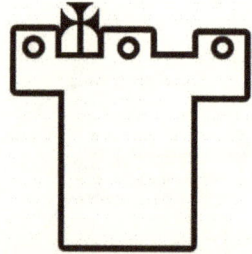

Alternate Seal of Halphas

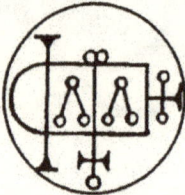

Traditional Seal of Malphas

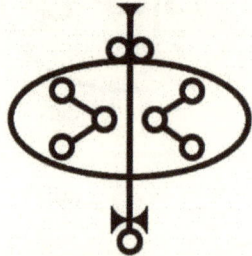

Alternate Seal of Malphas

(38.) HALPHAS

Halphas is the "white" twin of this set, and he appears in the form of a stock dove. He speaks with a hoarse voice. He is a spirit of war and defense, and his work is to build up towers, furnish them with ammunition and weapons, and to send warriors to places appointed.

His sigil looks like a siege tower.

(39.) MALPHAS

Malphas, the "black" twin of Halphas, appears like a crow. He also speaks with a hoarse voice.

He can build houses and high towers, like his brother, but he can also give you knowledge of your enemies' thoughts and desires and actions. His is a master of war strategy.

He gives good familiars.

He can be deceitful, since his mind is cunning. However, he is strongest and most loyal to a Master when he is called with 38 – Halphas.

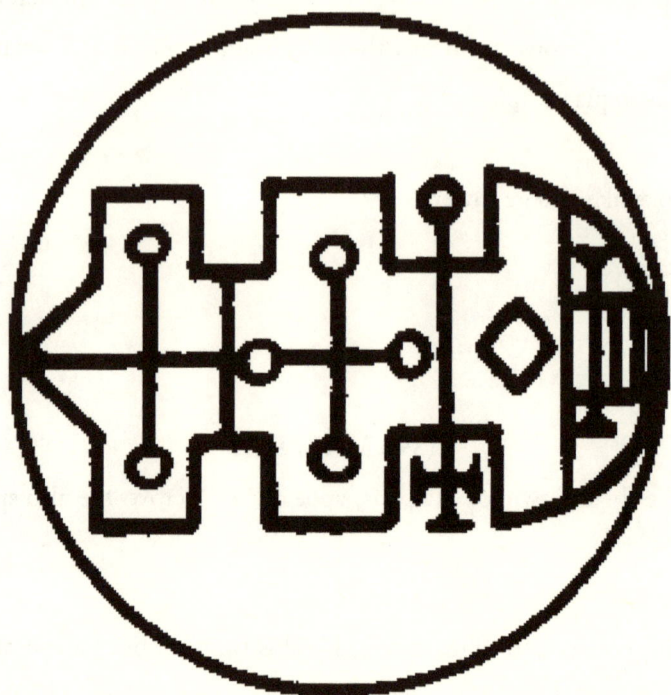

(40.) RAUM

Raum appears at first in the form of a crow. His office is to help his Master obtain money from the government (the "king's house").

He also destroys cities and the reputations of men.

Raum can also accurately divine the past, present, and future; and he can cause love between friends and foes.

His sigil represents the layout of a city. (Our alternate sigil is very loosely based on Indianapolis, the city nearest to us. Adapt the sigil to look like your own city, if you like.)

Alternate Sigil

"Focalor" © Natalie Black

(41.) FOCALOR

Focalor, a spirit of terrible weather, appears as a woman with gryphon's wings.

This spirit is very much like Oya. She has power over both winds and seas; and she can slay people using these elements. For instance, she can drown men and sink sturdy ships. However, she will not hurt any man or thing if she is commanded to the contrary by the Witch. But take care, because if you use her to stir up a storm and don't specify that nobody be killed, she may take her price.

She also has no delusions of returning to the Seventh Throne (the All) after 1,000 years, though the older texts claim she does.

Her anger is great, and her work is well-known. She is the rage of hurricanes and tropical storms. Currently, she likes best to be called "Katrina" – the brutal hurricane that decimated New Orleans in 2005.

Her sigil is lightning and storm clouds, as is Oya's veve.

Traditional Sigil

Alternate Sigil

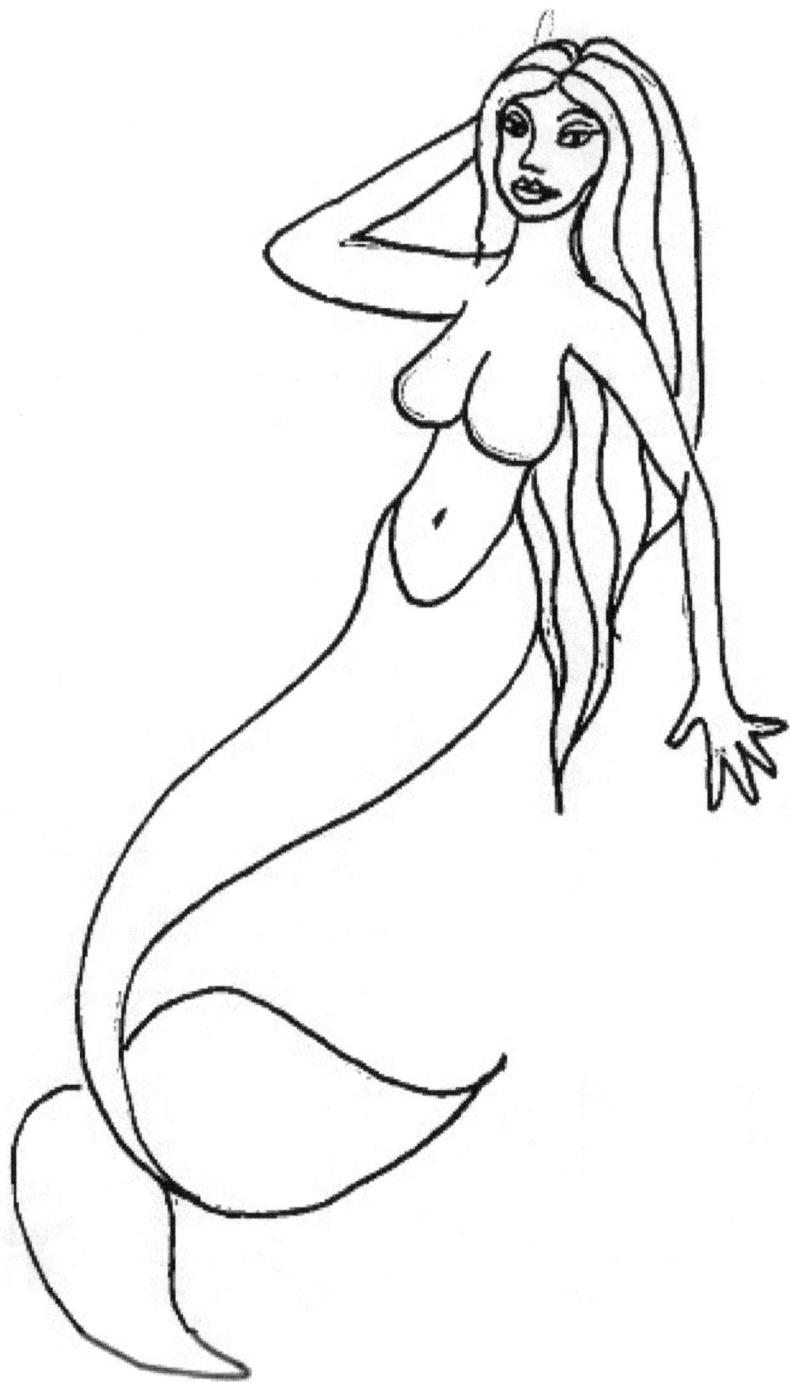

"Vepar" © 2013 Natalie Black

(42.) VEPAR

Vepar, another water spirit, appears like a mermaid, a siren, or the Lorelei. She changes forms and is usually quite beautiful. When she appears, she is singing. The sound is beautiful and not harmful to those who are meant to work with her, but it is dangerous to those who do not have an affinity with her.

Her office is to govern the waters and to guide warships. At the request of the Exorcist, she can cause the seas to be right stormy and to appear full of ships. She can also cause men to die in three days by putrefying, worm-infested wounds – or by inflicting them with trench foot.

She is very communicative, and her sigil represents waves, a mermaid, and ship.

Traditional Sigil   *Alternate Sigil*

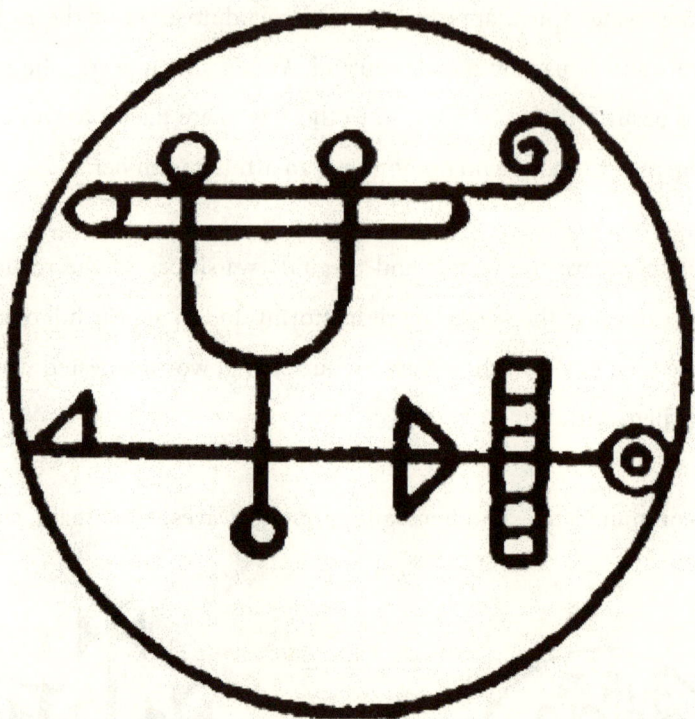

(43.) SABNOCK

He appears in the form of an armed soldier with a lion's head, riding on a pale-colored horse.

He is another spirit of war and defense. He can build high towers, castles and cities; and he furnishes them with armor and weapons. However, he is more suited to demolition and the destruction of fortresses.

Also, he can afflict men for many days with infected wounds.

He gives good familiars at the request of the Witch. He is best suited to work with engineers, architects, and weapon-smiths.

His sigil represents a man doing surveying work.

Alternate Sigil

(44.) SHAX

Shax, or "Chaz," appears in the form of a stock dove, speaking with a hoarse voice. Older texts say his voice is "subtle," but there is nothing subtle about Chaz. When in human form, he looks like a pimp, and he is most naturally aligned with those who exploit others for their own gain.

His skills include taking away the senses of any person (as if they were drugged – or insensible from orgasm) and to steal money from wealthy men.

He is a spirit who must first be commanded into a Pyramid, or else he will deceive the Witch.

He can discover all things that are hidden, if they are not kept by wicked spirits.

He gives good familiars, sometimes. There is no rhyme or reason to determine this, though.

Shax's sigil is, very obviously, male genitalia.

Alternate Sigil

(45.) VINE

Vine, or "Vinny," is a detective. His work is to discover hidden things, Witches and Mages, and to discern the truth. He can find out what has happened in the past, present, or future.

He is a "crooked" detective, though, and he might not always come forward honestly with the items or information he has found. You can bribe him quite successfully, of course, to share what he knows.

His sigil is a man's head wearing a crown.

Alternate Sigil

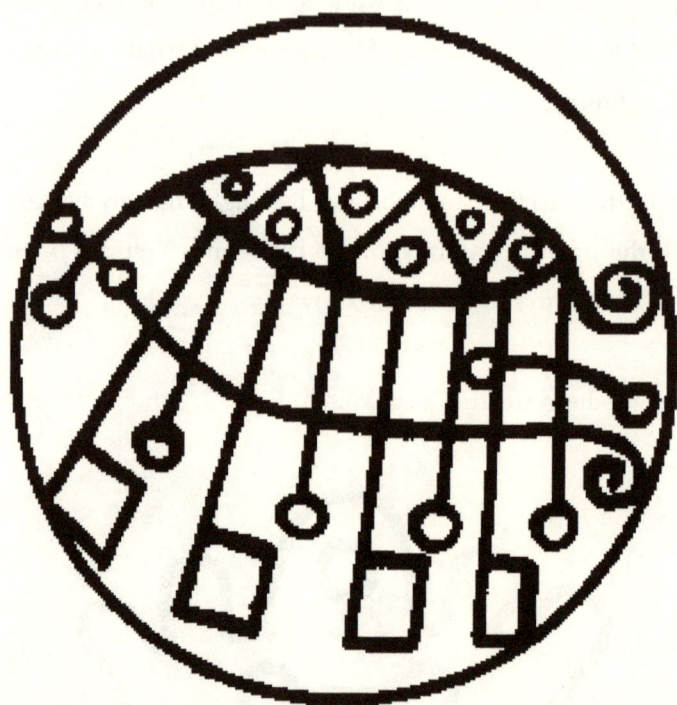

(46.) BIFRONS

Bifrons is like a frost giant in size and appearance (though he isn't truly a frost giant). He changes his own color between white and red, as it suits him in the moment.

He can make one knowing in astrology, geometry, and other arts and sciences. He teaches the properties of precious stones and woods.

He also sets wisps upon the graves of the dead.

Bifrons marks the beginning of a group of very learned spirits.

Alternate Sigil

(47.) UVALL

He appears in the shape of a large camel at first, but he will put on a human shape, if requested.

He speaks colloquial Coptic, and ONLY Coptic. However, he communicates most plainly via smoke, and he can communicate with a speaker of any language using this visual medium.

He can get a woman to love his Master (whether the Master is male or female), and he establishes friendships and alliances.

He divines all things.

His sigil is a camel.

Alternate Sigil

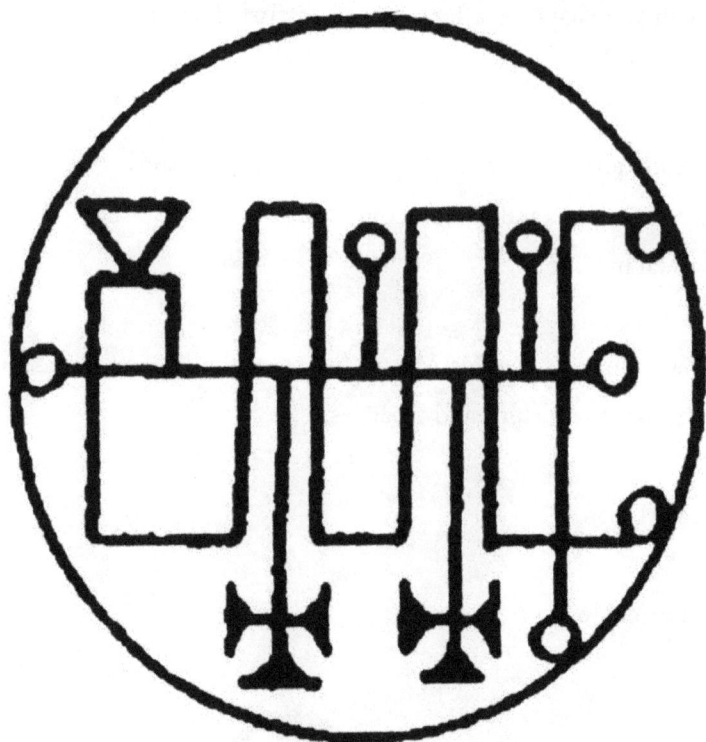

(48.) HAAGENTI

Pronounced: Ha'a-jenti.

He appears at first as mighty bull with gryphon's wings, and then as a man.

His office is to make men wise and to instruct them in many things.

He is also an alchemist, transmuting all metals into gold and changing wine into water (and vice versa).

His sigil is meant to represent alchemical equipment.

Alternate Sigil

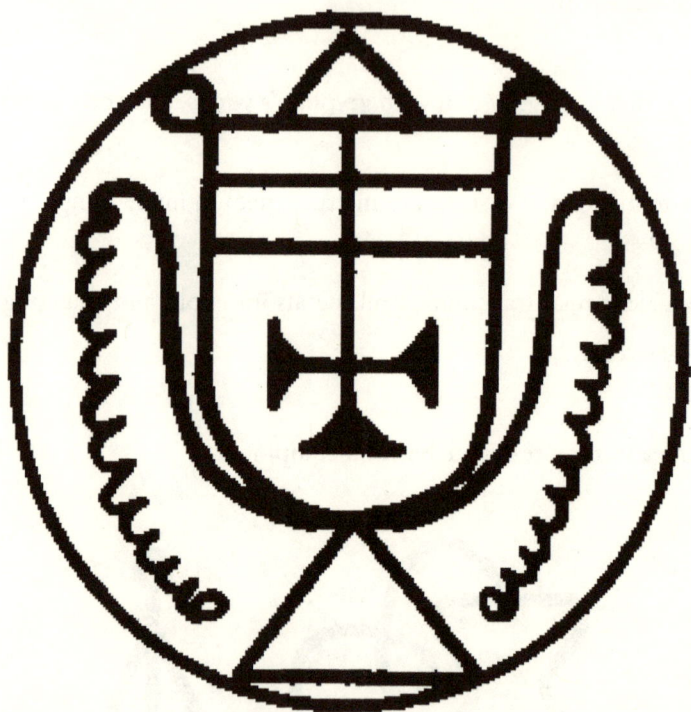

(49.) CROCELL

Pronounced: Crokelle.

He appears as an angel, and he speaks in riddles.

He teaches geometry and the liberal sciences.

He is very knowing in water magic, and can produce a sound like the rushing of many waters. He can also warm up waters and discover springs. He is excellent for those drawn to water-witching.

Crocell's sigil is an angelic cup.

Alternate Sigil

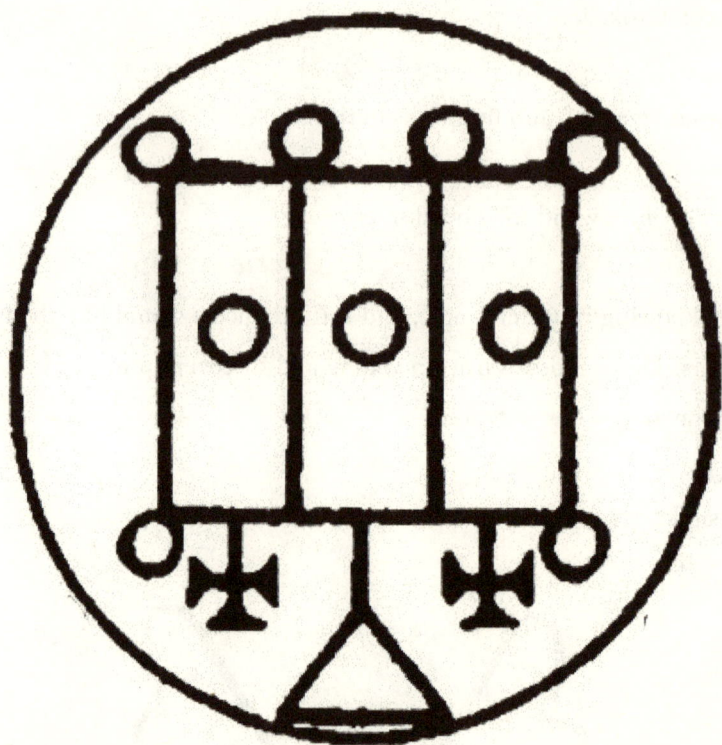

(50.) FURCAS

Furcas looks like a gruff and grumpy old man with a long beard and gray hair, riding upon a pale-colored horse, with a sharp weapon in his hand. His is indeed quite gruff, but he is not a dangerous spirit for the Master.

He is skilled in the arts of philosophy, astrology, rhetoric, logic, palmistry, and pyromancy; and he teaches these subjects in all their parts, and perfectly.

His sigil is a lamp.

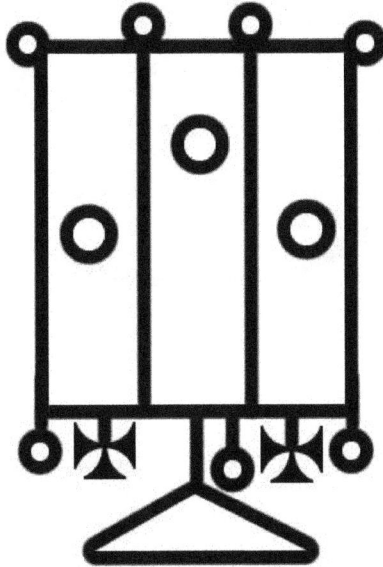

Alternate Sigil

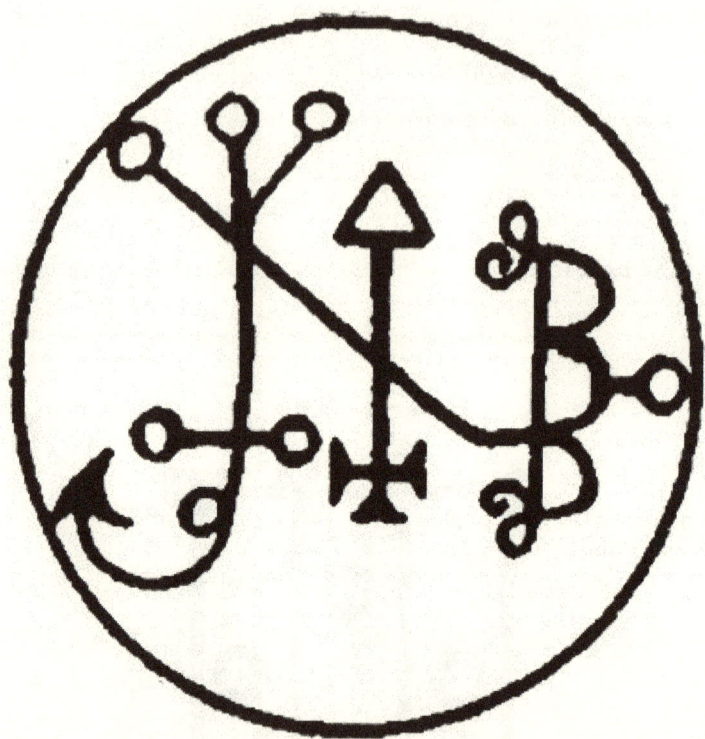

(51.) BALAM

Pronounced: Bala'am.

He is a terrible and powerful spirit who appears with three heads: those of bull, man, and ram. He has the tail of a serpent and flaming eyes. He rides upon a furious bear and carries a goshawk upon his fist.

He speaks with a hoarse voice, giving true answers of things past, present, and to come. He can help the Master to be witty.

Balam can be an unkind spirit, though he is not usually dangerous.

Alternate Sigil

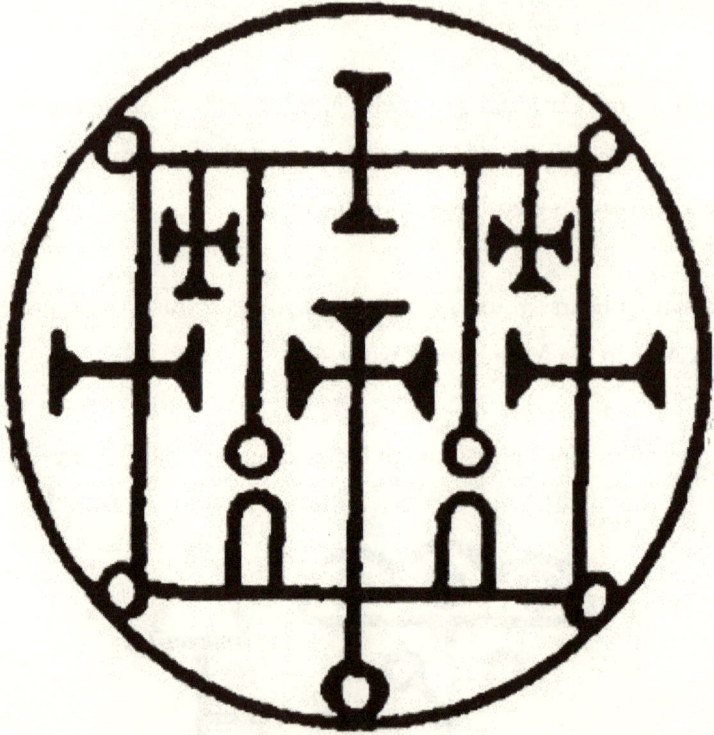

(52.) ALLOCES

Pronounced: Al-lokas.

He appears as a soldier riding upon a large horse. He has a red lion's face with flaming eyes. His voice is hoarse and very loud.

Alloces teaches the art of astronomy and all the liberal sciences.

He gives good familiars. Those spirits, though, like the Masters who work with Alloces, are often wise but not very kind.

His sigil is a wall.

Alternate Sigil

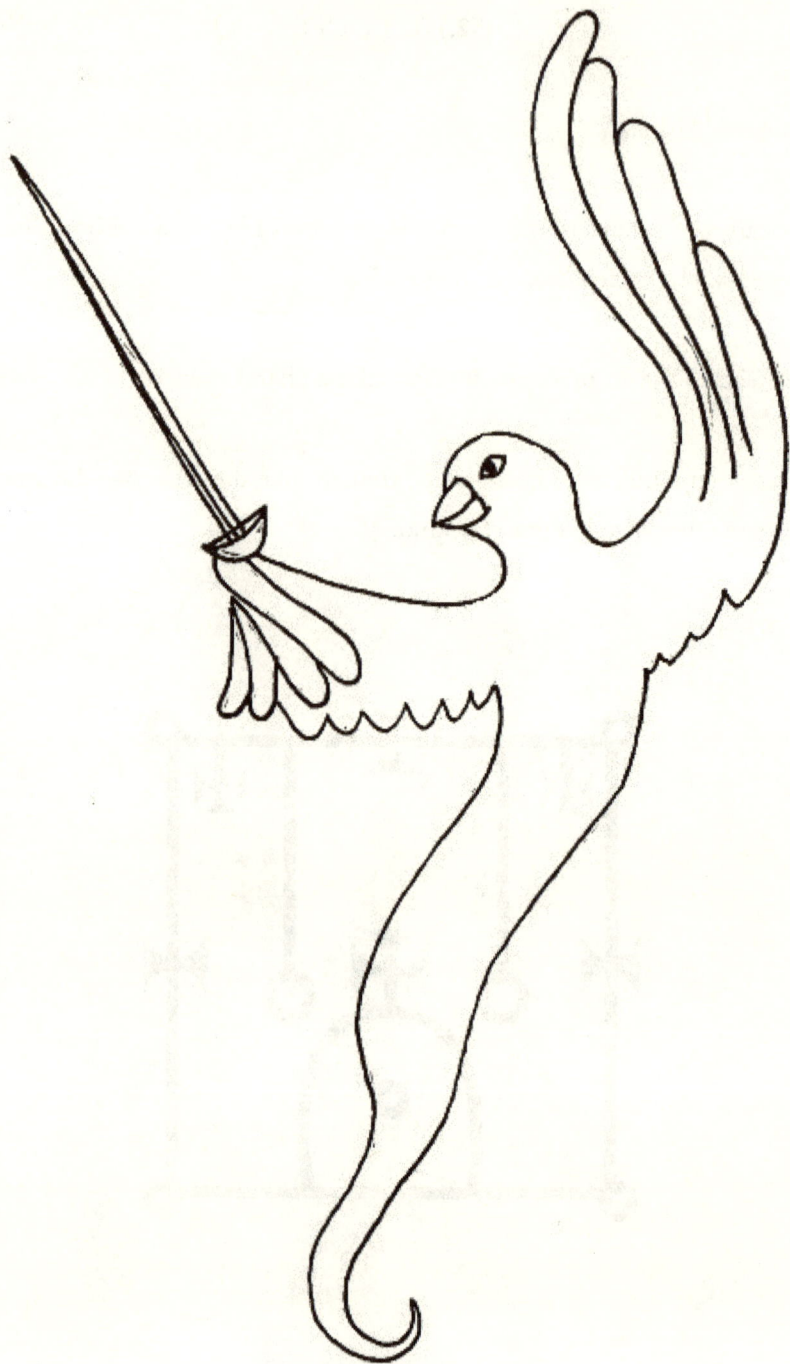

"Camio" © 2013 Natalie Black

(53.) CAMIO

Camio, or Caim, appears in the form of thrush at first, but then he changes into the form of a man carrying a sharp sword.

He communicates well through fire and ember scrying. He is talented at argumentation and debate, making him an excellent familiar for lawyers.

He helps the Master find meaning in the voices of birds, cattle, dogs, and other animals. He also helps the Master via auditory messages in water (like scrying, but aurally, not visually). He gives true answers of things to come.

His sigil is represents the thrush.

Traditional Sigil

Alternate Sigil

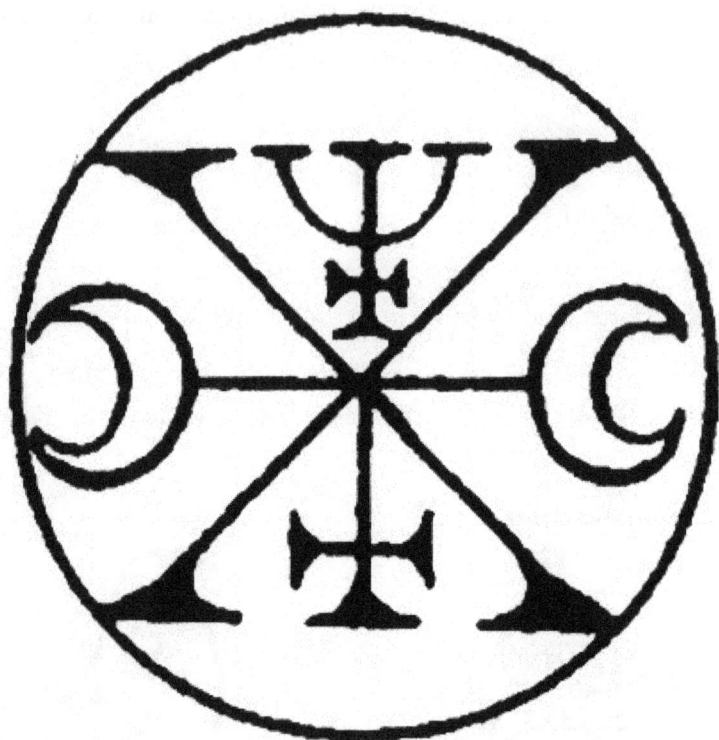

(54.) MURMUR

Murmur's name originates from the murmuring or mumbling sounds he makes when speaking. He appears as a gryphon wearing a crown.

Previous editions of this Key have indicated that a host of men and blaring trumpets preceed him; however, he is truthfully very quiet in demeanor and speech.

His teaches philosophy perfectly.

Also, he aids the Master in communicating with the Dead, both by bringing spirits to the Master and by facilitating conversation and understanding.

He is very communicative in his own way – usually via a visual medium such as scrying or vision questing.

Alternate Sigil

"Orobas" © 2013 Natalie Black

(55.) OROBAS

Orobas appears at first like a horse before taking the shape of a man. He can divine all things, and he also brings dignity, honor, and praise to the Master. (Orobas is, himself, a very popular spirit; and he can help the Master find her own sort of popularity and renown.)

He is very wise and can help the Master understand spiritual matters and Mysteries. He is very faithful to his Master, and he offers protection from harmful spirits.

His sigil is meant to represent portals.

Traditional Sigil   *Alternate Sigil*

"Gamori" by John Birkel © 2013

(56.) GREMORY

Gremory, or Gamori, is a strong, beautiful, and powerful woman with red hair riding upon a black camel. She is related to Lilith and to Babalon in a great many ways.

She is an accurate and powerful diviner, and she helps the Witch develop her psychic abilities. She can even help the Master uncover treasures (both spiritual and physical).

She works well with women who identify as lesbian or bisexual, and she assists both men and women in obtaining the affections of women, whether young or old.

Gremory's sigil is a veiled and crowned woman.

Traditional Sigil

Alternate Sigil

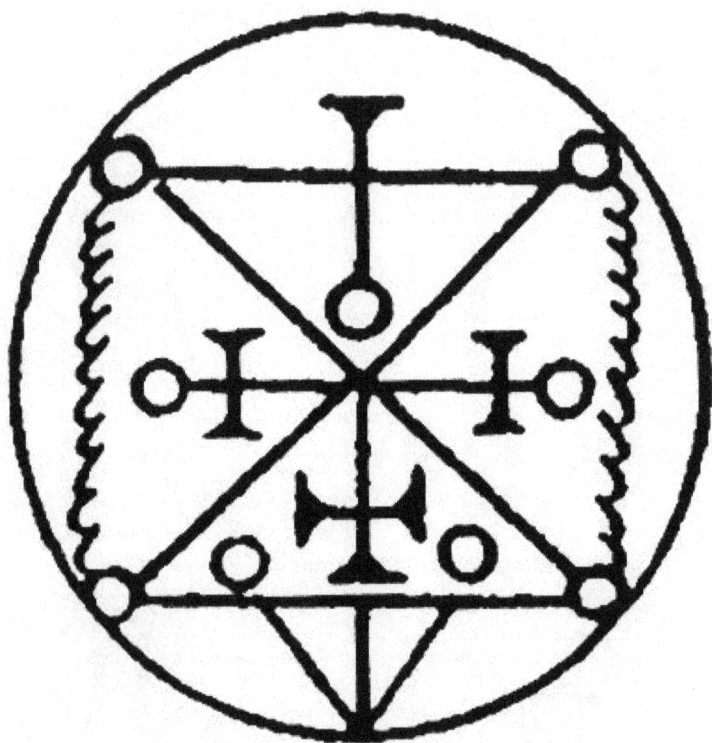

(57.) OSE

Oso, Ose, or Voso. He is known as Ochosi (Oxochis, Ososi) within Yoruban-derived religious systems.

Oso is a shaman, and he very often appears in a state of partial transformation, showing his ability to shape-shift. In this sense, he can change a person into any shape they wish, even to the extent that they believe for a time that they are that animal in truth. The animal most commonly associated with him is the leopard or jaguar.

His can make one cunning in the liberal sciences, and he gives true answers of secret and divine things.

He (and his Masters) often work with entheogens and hallucinogens in order to find meaning and wisdom.

His sigil is a leopard skin.

Alternate Sigil

"Ami" © 2013 Natalie Black

(58.) AMY

Amy is also called Ami (which means "friend" in French and shows the familiar nature of this spirit). Ami is one of the more well-known Witches' familiars from medieval texts and witch trial records (being noted in the trial of Rebecca Jones and in the list of familiars noted Witch-Finder General, Matthew Hopkins).

This spirit appears as fire – neither masculine nor feminine, neither good nor bad.

Hir office is to make one very learned in astronomy and the liberal sciences.

Ami gives good familiars.

Hir sigil is a creature of fire.

Traditional Sigil

Alternate Sigil

(59.) ORIAX

Oriax comes in the shape of a man with a lion's face, and he often appears with many legs. He has unnaturally long and slender fingers. He is another inter-dimensional traveler (like Purson). It is not inaccurate to call him an alien.

He teaches the properties and powers of stars, and he assists the Master with understand astrology in great detail.

He also transforms men, and gives honor and favor to his Master. He is very helpful and very friendly.

His sigil looks like a thin angel.

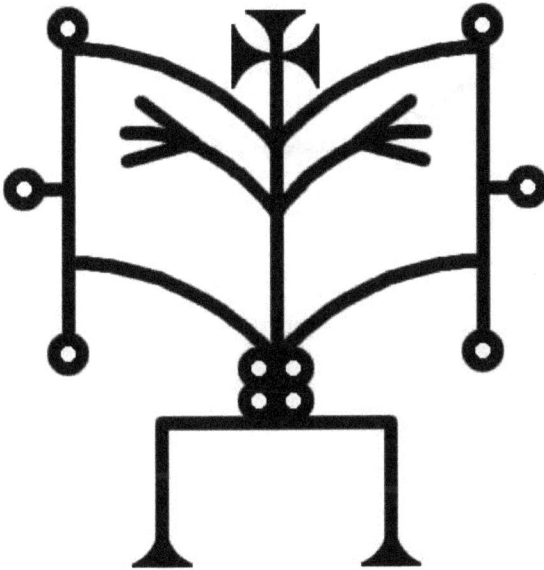

Alternate Sigil

(60.) VAPULA

Vapula, or Naphula, appears as an angel.

She is very prim, but polite. She is a friendly and feminine spirit who can help men obtain the love of women.

She assists the Master in all handicrafts and professions, and she teaches philosophy and science.

Her sigil looks like an angel bearing a heart.

Alternate Sigil

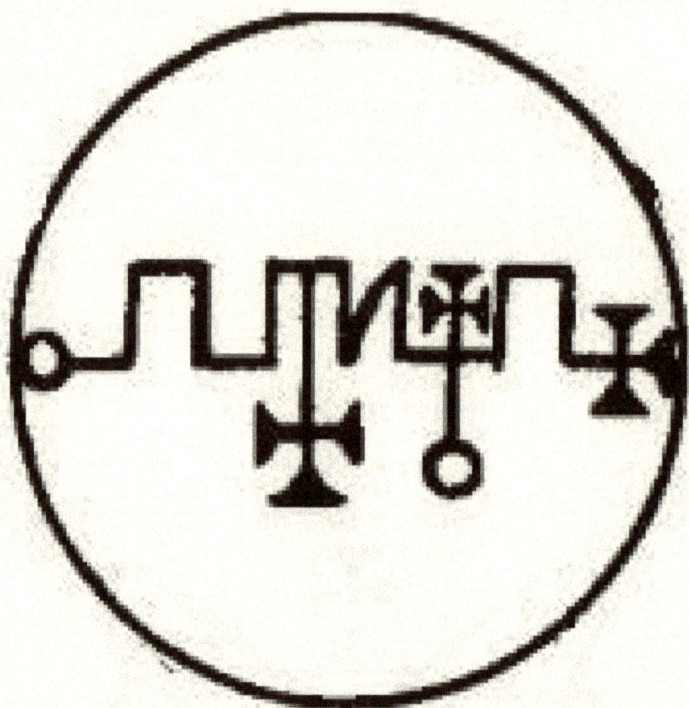

(61.) ZAGAN

Zagan, or Dagon, appears as a bull with gryphon's wings before assuming the shape of a man.

Dagon was a semitic God of fish and grain, and he may have been the head of the Philistines' pantheon.

Zagan's chief function is to transform things – water into wine, wine into water, blood into wine, metal into money, and foolish people into wise ones.

His sigil is a snake.

Alternate Sigil

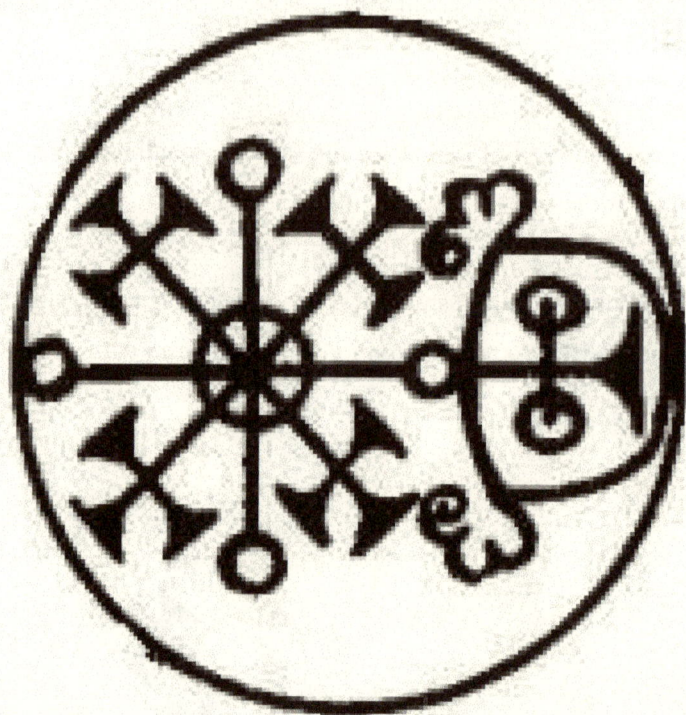

(62.) VALAK

Valak is a mighty, old, and wise dragon; though he sometimes appears as a child riding upon a dragon.

He is wise but volatile, like a child with tantrums. He poses some threat to the Mage in the sense that those who work with him tend to develop hubris.

He helps the Master work with serpent energy – the ley lines within the Earth and the kundalini within the body.

Valak's sigil is meant to be a dragon.

Alternate Sigil

(63.) ANDRAS. – DO NOT CALL

Andras is a manslayer who comes in the form of a black angel with a raven's head, riding upon a black wolf and brandishing a bright, sharp sword.

There is no value in calling him, as his only purpose is to cause discord.

His sigil is meant to look like a devil-fish.

"Haures" © 2013 Natalie Black

(64.) HAURES

Pronounced: Horus.

The spirit Haures is known to Thelemites as Ra-Hoor Khuit, and he appears to those who call him as a mighty, terrible, and strong man. His eyes are flaming and his countenance is terrifying.

He gives true answers of the past, present, and future. He will also talk of the creation of the world, of divinity, and of how he and other spirits "fell."

Earlier texts say that he will lie if he is not called within the Pyramid. He doesn't lie. He is very honest, often saying things the Master doesn't want to hear.

He destroys and burns up the enemies of the Witch; and he will not suffer his Master to be tempted by any other being, spirit or otherwise.

Traditional Sigil

Alternate Sigil

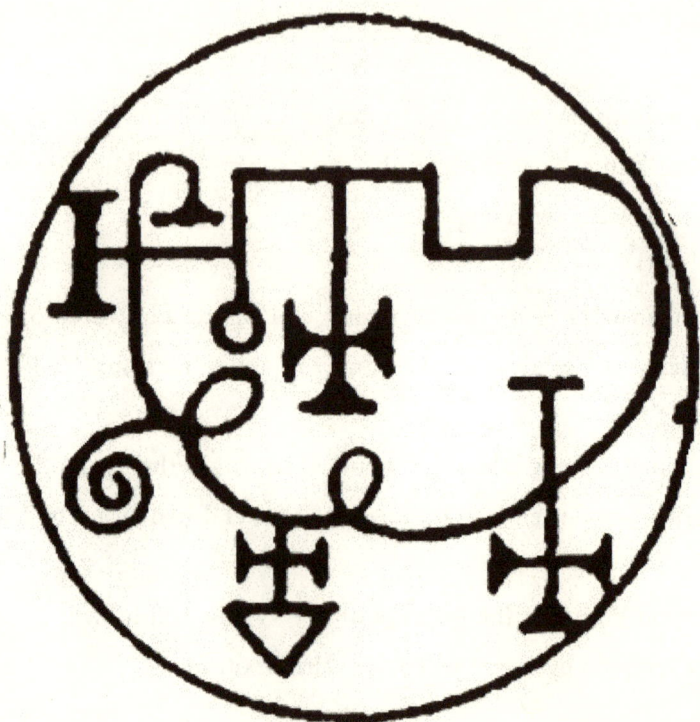

(65.) ANDREALPHUS

Before changing into a human shape, he appears like a peacock while making sounds like the cries of a peacock.

He can teach geometry, astronomy, and the analytical subtleties related to these sciences. He is a wonderful spirit for analysts, mathematicians, and scientists.

He can also help the Master with shapeshifting into bird forms.

His seal is meant to represent the brain.

Alternate Sigil

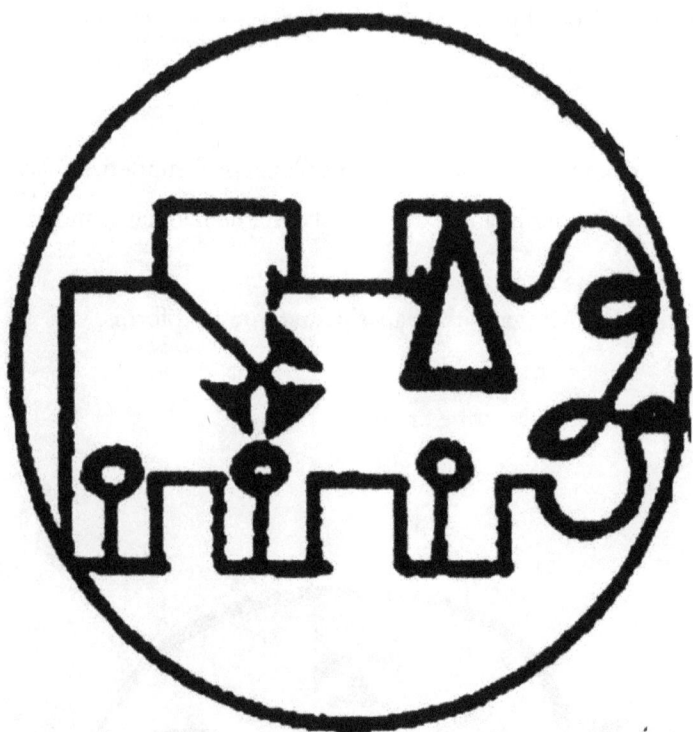

(66.) KAMARIS

Kamaris appears as an African warrior riding a large black horse.

He rules over all the spirits originating in Africa. (A little bit of etymological research uncovers the fact that KAMA is a root word common among African languages. The Biblical book of Genesis refers to the African continent as Kam.) He was once a very strong spirit; however, he has lost considerable strength due to decreasing magical contact with mortals.

He teaches grammar, logic, and rhetoric; and he can discover treasures and lost or hidden objects.

His seal is a horse.

Alternate Sigil

"Amdusias" © 2013 Natalie Black

(67.) AMDUSIAS

Amdusias, or Amdukias, is a very popular spirit among Mages, appearing in the form of a (slightly drunk) unicorn. Sleipnir is a well-known Norse manifestation of this same spirit. When he appears in human form, he prefers the face and form of Jim Morrison.

He teaches music and is a natural ally to musicians, composers, and poets.

He also teaches tree magic and the lore of tree alphabets – like the Norse Runes and Celtic Ogham.

He gives excellent familiars.

His sigil is reminiscent of a unicorn.

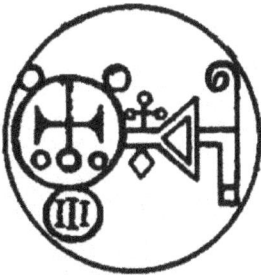

Traditional Sigil   *Alternate Sigil*

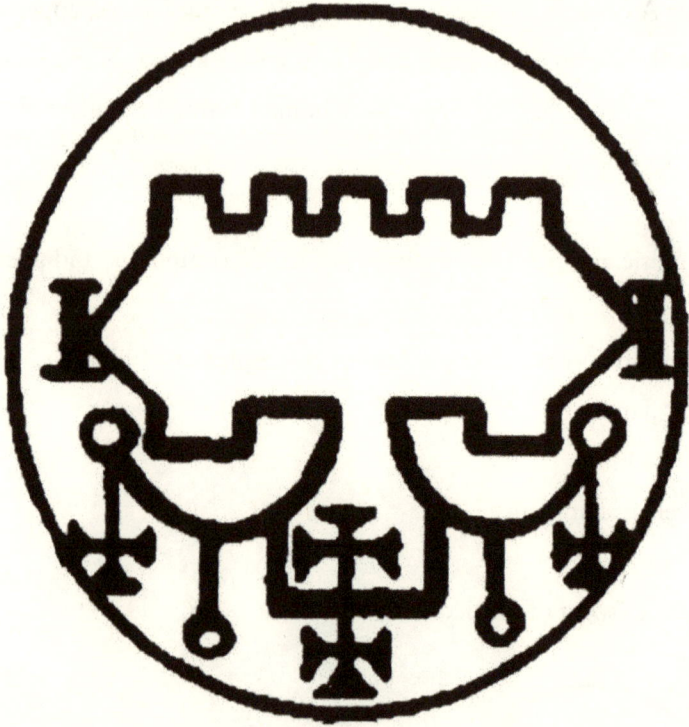

(68.) BELIAL. –DO NOT CALL

He is a leader amongst the harmful spirits of the Legion, and our spirit guide actually pleaded with us not to discuss him. He causes fear among the spirits, and his mission is deceit. In fact, we were told, "He *is* deceit."

Older texts tell us that he appears as an angel in a fiery chariot and that he was one of the Fallen who came to Earth to be with the daughters of man. He is said to give good familiars (though that is presumably only to those Mages who desire harm and revel in lies) and to bring accolades and honors to the Master.

A contemporary form he enjoys is that of a rough and terrifying motorcycle gang member.

He delights in brutal torment.

His sigil is a cruelly-devised helmet or mask.

"Decarabia" © 2013 Natalie Black

(69.) DECARABIA

Pronounced: Dek-arabia.

She appears first as a five-pointed star and then takes the form of a beautiful woman. She is like Aradia or Herodias, the first Witch, daughter of the Sun and Moon.

She is talented in the art of vision questing and scrying, and she can discover the properties and wisdom of birds and precious stones. She particularly assists the Mage in the arts of bird and cloud scrying.

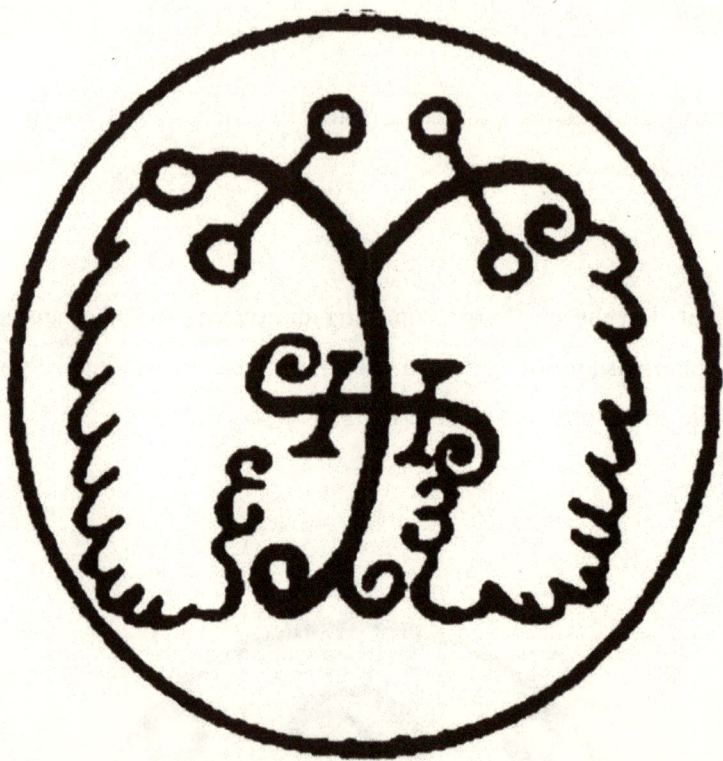

(70.) SEERE

He is a beautiful man riding upon a winged horse.

He is not on the Do NOT CALL list, but Masters should use care when working with him. He is a powerful and cunning servant of the Adversary. He is very helpful and friendly to the Mage in life, but his goal is to bring deceased spirits under the power of the Adversary. He attempts to make bargains with the Mage to this end, using the trust he has gained from his helpfulness as a sort of currency.

He does practically anything the Master wishes: appear and disappear as called; make things happen for the Master's benefit; bring objects into and out of the Master's possession, as desired. He works very quickly, and he can discover the answers to most questions.

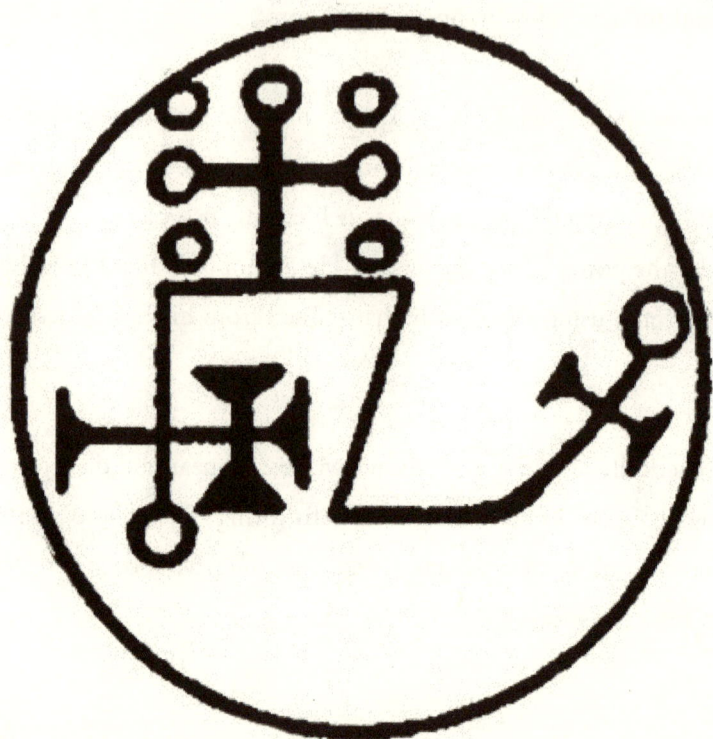

(71.) DANTALION

Pronounced: Dan-tallion.

This spirit can appear as anyone, male or female. S/he is often seen with a book in hir hand.

S/he can teach all arts and sciences, tell all secrets, and discover any person's thoughts.

This spirit is very stubborn in demeanor and doesn't make a friendly familiar. If s/he does work with you, s/he will want your sole attention and loyalty, as s/he doesn't play well with other spirits.

Hir sigil is like a minister in a pulpit (or a magistrate at a stand).

Alternate Sigil

(72.) ANDROMALIUS

Andromalius is a spirit of justice, appearing with a serpent in his hands.

He can bring back a thief and the goods he stole, discover lies and wrong-doing, and punish the wicked. He can also discover hidden treasures, both physical and metaphysical in nature.

He is a good companion to those born in the sign of Libra.

His sigil is a set of scales and a serpent.

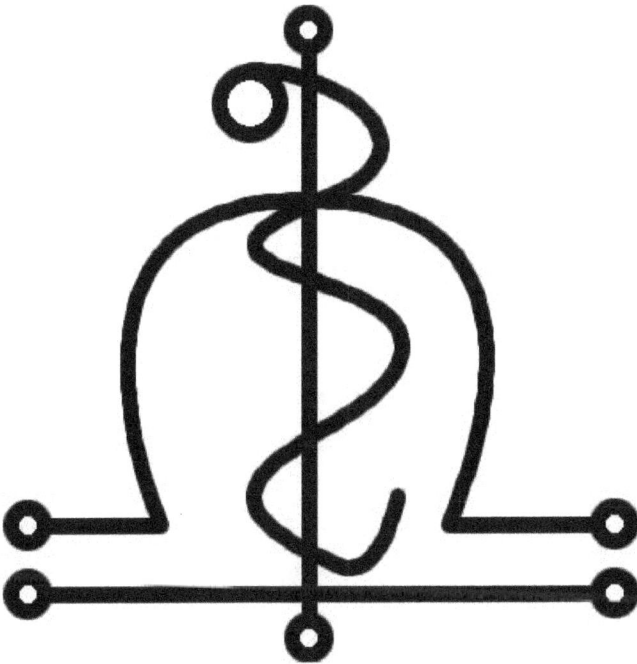

Alternate Sigil